Dear J.R. — may you [...] from you Best [...] Laurel Clark 2/23/2013

Intuitive Dreaming

by **Laurel Clark**
D.M., D.D., B.A.

SOM Publishing
Windyville, MO 65783
U.S.A.

© August 2012
by the School of Metaphysics No. 100200

Cover design by Joseph Leaderbrand

Interior design and layout by Karen Mosby

Ten digit ISBN: 0-944386-70-9
Thirteen digit ISBN: 9780944386705

Library of Congress Control No. 2012944996
PRINTED IN THE UNITED STATES OF AMERICA

If you desire to learn more about the research
and teachings in this book, write to

School of Metaphysics World Headquarters,
Windyville, Missouri 65783

Visit us on the internet at www.som.org

*I dedicate this book to dreamers everywhere for the courage
to explore intuition and the inner levels of consciousness.
May we all bring about a more sensitive, open-hearted, and
connected world through sharing our dream discoveries.*

Table of Contents

Introduction

I don't know when I remembered my first dream. I do know that as a child, I relished the experience of being in the dream world and had some favorite dreams, especially the ones with houses ... the rooms with secret passageways, hidden rooms, finding lost treasures.

When I was a junior in college at the University of Michigan, I was taking a writing class as part of a program called the New England Literature Program. We went to New Hampshire for six weeks in late spring, lived in the woods, read the works of transcendentalist writers like Henry David Thoreau and Ralph Waldo Emerson, fiction of New England authors like Nathaniel Hawthorne, Emily Dickinson, and Robert Frost. We kept our own journals and discussed them in small writing groups.

One of my friends wrote beautiful poetry that she read in our group. I was envious. I wrote poetry, too, but mine seemed stilted, with words that expressed ideas or emotions. Her poems were rich in sensual imagery. When I asked her where she came up with such evocative metaphors, she said, "From my dreams."

At that time, I had little memory of dreams. The only dreams I remembered were occasional nightmares that woke me up, sweating and afraid to go back to sleep. I asked Cris how she was able to capture her dreams and she suggested I write them down.

"How can I write them down if I don't remember?" I persisted. She told me to put my journal by the bed and tell myself before going to sleep that I wanted to remember and record my dreams. She insisted that simply by wanting to, and having the journal within reach with a pen, I would begin to remember.

She was right. I have been keeping a dream journal ever since.

Two years later, I discovered the School of Metaphysics. On the first night of class, our teacher gave an introduction to dreams, instructing us to keep a dream journal and to bring it to class the following week. She said she would teach us the language of dreams and we would soon learn to interpret our own.

By that time, I had already filled several notebooks with dreams that I had no idea how to interpret. It was gratifying to begin to decipher the messages, and quite amazing to me to learn how accurate they were.

The School of Metaphysics (SOM) study is a comprehensive program that teaches people spiritual disciplines. Dream work is an integral part of the study, beginning with learning the Universal Language of Mind[1], applying the dream messages through visualization to cause change and understanding, and progressing to inner level work such as dream classes, astral projection, and lucid dreaming.

Learning to record dreams was just the first step in a long journey of self-discovery. Once remembering, recording, and interpreting dreams became a daily spiritual practice, I found that my attention was honed to note any references to dreams in the news. In the late 1970's and early 1980's when I was a student new to metaphysics, the references to dreams in mainstream media were rare. When there was an article in a popular magazine, like *Reader's Digest* or *Psychology Today*, it appeared that the quoted dream experts were from an organization called (at that time) the Association for the Study of Dreams.

I was curious to know more about this association, but while actively pursuing my education with the School of Metaphysics and volunteering as a teacher, director, and area director, the time was not right. I graduated from the course of study in 1994 and continued to serve as a teacher and area director. In 2006 I accepted a position as President of SOM to be able to reach more people and broaden the scope of my teaching.

In 2008, within a week, three separate people told me that I should attend the conference of the International Association for the Study of Dreams (IASD) that was to be held in Montreal. They thought it would be good for me to learn about the organization and to represent the School of Metaphysics. I'd known about the organization since the early 1980's, and now three people, in the same week, were encouraging me to attend the conference. Seemed like more than a coincidence!

I decided to attend; in fact, I sent in a proposal to present some research the School of Metaphysics had recently conducted on the moon's effect on dreams.[2] My friend Sheila Benjamin, also a long-time teacher with the School of Metaphysics, was also a presenter. We went as pioneers, to learn about the IASD, to meet new people, and to expand the realm of our understanding of dreams.

That year Christine Lemley and Viki Anderson were there to film episodes of *Dreamtime*, a television series on dreams to be broadcast on PBS.[3] That seemed like a notable synchronicity, since I had recently met Christine and Viki and helped them develop the series pilot. My student Amy Pawlus and I were instrumental in researching and documenting the importance of dreams for their proposal to PBS. Amy and I were interviewed as the dream experts for the pilot that was filmed at WFYI in Indianapolis.

I was enchanted with this wonderful, diverse group of people. They are scientists, artists, psychologists, ministers, musicians, yoga practitioners, energy workers, historians, educators, mystics, lucid dreamers, and everyday folks who keep dream journals, exploring their meaning in many different ways. The common element among the people was, and is, an interest in dreams.

Being at that conference stimulated me to pay even closer attention to my dreams. My recall and awareness of intuitive dreams has deepened since I participated in the 2008 conference. In the fall of that year, I took part in the online PsiberDreaming Conference (PDC). This is a dreamer's paradise! People from all over the world spend two weeks immersed in reading online presentations, discussing the papers, their own dreams, playing in the imaginative world of the Outer Inn (a virtual inn that inspires creativity and telepathic connections) and developing intuitive skills with dream contests such as telepathy, precognition, and mutual dreaming.

The presence of intuitive connections is very strong because people concentrate on dreams so dramatically during that time.

Often, the participants report dreaming of other people who are taking part in the conference (even if they have never met in person) and have mutual dreams.

This book is a compilation of some of these experiences I've had with dream telepathy, precognition, mutual dreams, and visitations. Several of the chapters are adaptations of presentations I have given both in-person at the IASD Conferences and for the PsiberDreaming Conferences. Some are adaptations of lectures I have given in cities where I travel and teach with the School of Metaphysics.

For those of you who like to skim books and skip around while you read, you may enjoy the chapters one at a time. Most of them stand alone so you don't have to read them in order because they do not follow a linear sequence. Much like intuition! In fact, one of the most profound intuitive dreams I had on the evening of September 11, 2001, is described in two different chapters. Sometimes a story is worth telling more than once...

I hope that you will be inspired to explore the inner world of your own psyche that is revealed in dreams. Whether your dreams are spiritual, or healing, or give you foreshadowing of future events, whether you dream of past lives or share dreams with others, receive inspiration for art or music or poetry, the realm of the dream world is magical and powerful.

May you deepen your connections with people all over the world who love to dream.

What is a Dream?

What is a dream? This may seem like a simple question, but the answers are multi-faceted.

For over 30 years I have kept a dream journal. As a School of Metaphysics student, I learned that dreams communicate truth from the subconscious mind. People who listen to dreams learn to heed their own inner teacher. Keeping a dream journal is a wonderful resource for evaluating soul development. In fact, Dr. Barbara O'Guinn Condron, a dream expert, spiritual teacher, and author, calls a dream journal one's "spiritual autobiography." I love that.

My dreaming experience has evolved over time. At first, I learned to view dreams as messages from the inner self that can be interpreted. The School of Metaphysics teaches dream interpretation through understanding the Universal Language of Mind, a metaphorical language of symbols that resonate with the spiritual self.[1]

While all dreams can be interpreted as messages about the dreamer's waking state of awareness, some dreams are also experiences in other dimensions. When we dream with other people, meet with those who have died, travel to the future or the past, or receive telepathic communications, the dream-happening gives us a taste of existence that is beyond our everyday waking reality.

In recent years, I have met people who approach dreams from many different perspectives. The International Association for the Study of Dreams (IASD) brings people together from all walks of life who explore their own dreams, who use dreams in therapeutic settings, who study what happens in the brain when we dream, and who write dream-inspired poetry, compose dream-inspired music, or dance the stories told in dreams.

Some question whether dreams have meaning at all. My appreciation for the IASD is the open-mindedness of researchers to learn from each other regarding this basic query, "What is a dream and what meaning can we derive from dream work?" Brain scientists view dreams as a neurological event, a function of physiological changes that occur when a person sleeps. Metaphysicians view dreams as a consciousness event, in which the neurological changes are effects, rather than the cause, for the altered state of consciousness we call a dream.

One's view of the Self influences our understanding of dreams and the dream experience. What do we mean when we say "I" in the statement, "I had a dream"? Are we talking about the physical body/brain "I"? The conscious ego "I"? The spiritual beyond-the-physical "I"?

This larger question dictates how we approach the meaning of dreams. Some people view dreams as a way of refreshing the brain and body. Some view it as a means of problem solving. Mystics and people who practice spiritual disciplines view dreams as a doorway into states of consciousness that awaken us to a larger "Self" than we ordinarily experience.

This book is an exploration of my own experience with the self, the Self, mind and consciousness. Intuitive dreaming, in my world, brings comfort and fulfillment. It nourishes the soul. Some dreams feel more "real" than the physical world, because they awaken us to the inter-connectedness of life. Honoring a dream is a way to pay homage to the divine.

As a metaphysician I understand that there is a reality above and beyond the physical senses and physical world. This "meta" or "beyond" physical existence is the realm of metaphysics. At the School of Metaphysics, the definition of "intuition" is the direct grasp of truth. Viewing a subject or thing intellectually is to view it by being apart from it. Intuition comes from direct experience.

When one has an intuitive dream, sometimes called a psi dream, there is a palpable shift of attention. Some people call this state "supernatural" or "paranormal," meaning that it is not physical. I have learned through participating in the PsiberDreaming Conferences at the IASD that in the field of dream and psi research there are commonly accepted terms to differentiate waking reality and dreaming reality. Researcher E. W. Kellogg III, Ph.D. in his essay, *"Paranormal Phenomena Frequently Asked Questions"* defines some of the abbreviations used to describe "reality":

"When you refer to 'reality', what do you mean?

Mainstream scientists frequently use the term 'reality' as a synonym for the 'physical universe.' Nevertheless, according to modern neurophysiologists, the 'physical universe' as such exists only hypothetically, as they affirm that we can only indirectly experience it through neural simulations of it (hence IBEs [In the Body Experience]). According to this theory, the 'physical reality' that we actually experience seems only an imperfect simulation *and abstraction of a physical universe whose existence we can only infer, and never directly confirm. In contrast to this point of view, I take a descriptive attitude when using the term reality. From a phenomenological point of view, the term reality refers to the world of direct experience, the world in which we live. From this viewpoint, **DR**, **LDR**, **OBR**, [Dream Reality, Lucid Dream Reality, Out of Body Reality] and **WPR** [Waking Physical Reality] simply make up subset realities of a greater experiential reality (**ER**), that we directly experience."*[2]

I appreciate Dr. Kellogg's description because it points out that one defines "reality" according to a viewpoint. Questions that arise in the study of dreams remind me of those that surface when exploring religion. In both disciplines one can approach the subject intellectually, with abstract ideas, and can seek answers intuitively, through direct perception. In the field of religion, this is the relationship between scholars and mystics.

This is not necessarily a dichotomy: people can receive knowledge with the intellect and through direct experience. In the field of dreams, some academic theorists are stimulated to research dreams because of their own experience; sometimes dreamers with "extraordinary" dreams become curious about the cause for their paranormal dreams. Some volunteer to become research subjects and add to the body of knowledge that enhances the theory.

The IASD integrates these approaches by bringing together academics and mystics, along with artists, musicians, counselors, and anyone else who loves to dream! At the conferences, both in-person and online, "psi" dreaming contests test dreamers' acumen. Dreamers learn through self-evaluations how to identify, and describe, their own intuitive processes. This advances research individually and collectively.

For the purpose of this book, a dream is defined as the experience of the Self when one is asleep. The "I" or the whole Self includes spirit, soul, and body. It includes Infinite Intelligence, Infinite Energy, Infinite Manifestation, and beyond all of that, Infinite Being.

I understand "reality" to include more than the physical

universe. We are all related in a kind of spiritual eco-system. Thought affects manifestation, and the environment affects our thoughts and moods. One person's attitudes and actions influence another. All of this is reflected in our dreaming experience.

One purpose for writing this book is to inspire people to explore their own dreams and intuition. How many people have discounted their intuitive experiences because they thought (or were told) it was "only" a dream, meaning, "It was not real"? Or they second-guessed an intuitive hunch because they didn't want others to think they were crazy?

Learning to integrate inner knowledge with the judgments of the brain is both an art and a science. It takes practice to develop discernment, to distinguish truth from falsehood, perception from imagination. It requires objectivity. In many cases, attachment to ideas or emotions may cloud the clear perception of intuitive knowing. I know two women who were assaulted because they denied an intuitive sense of danger they felt in the presence of a man of another race. In both cases, the women did not want the man, and other people, to think that they were racially prejudiced. So they ignored their own inner sense of danger and walked into a situation — an elevator in one case, and a deserted street in another — that harmed them.

Intuition is not always related to danger, despite the way it is often portrayed in the media. Responding to intuition can bring good fortune. I was able to save someone's life because of a telepathic connection in a dream. In another case, a friend found a valuable heirloom ring when she listened to her deceased grandmother who appeared in a dream telling her to look in the drawer where it was hidden.

Wouldn't it make our lives easier and richer if we all recognized that dreams are real? My hope is that this book aids you to open the door to your own dreamworld, or, if you have already walked through the door, to explore new passages with fellow dream-travelers.

I believe that our collective reality can become much more whole through understanding these nocturnal adventures. Let us all use our dreams to become happy, healthy, and holy.

Intuitive
Dreaming

Inner Level Communication

I have absolutely no fear of death. From my near-death research and my personal experiences, death is, in my judgment, simply a transition into another kind of reality. — *Dr. Raymond Moody*

Most people fear death. Although we know that death is inevitable, there is often a difference between what we believe intellectually and what we experience emotionally. Why is this so? It would seem that such a universal experience could be met with acceptance. Instead, at least in American culture, we often think of death as a failure. Some people don't even want to talk about it.

Elisabeth Kubler-Ross, author of **On Death and Dying**, identified five stages people go through in the process of dying: denial, anger, bargaining, depression, and acceptance.[1] The first stage, denial, is prevalent in Western culture. People with terminal illness are often counseled to "fight" the disease. Family members may even be advised not to tell the loved one that death is imminent.

To complicate matters, with so many medical treatments now available, there is much ambiguity concerning life and death decisions. For example, do we have to go through surgery, or chemotherapy, or take medications just because they are available? Is it "giving up" if one chooses not to live with a respirator or feeding tube? If a person whose health is declining decides to let the body go, does that mean he or she has failed?

These are questions facing not only the person who is ill or dying, but also their family and friends. In some cases it is more difficult for those who survive, because they need to live with the choices. Many people have regrets after a loved one dies, either wondering if they made the right choice to turn down a medical procedure or regretting having chosen a medical procedure which resulted in pain, complications, or death.

How Dreams Can Help

Being attentive to our dreams can help tremendously in understanding and even eliminating the fear of death. Dreams awaken us to the reality that there is experience beyond the physical body. They can give us a taste of life on the "other side," thus stimulating curiosity rather than dread.

Dreams can give us comfort, helping those who remain alive to know that they are not really separated from their loved ones who die. They may also help to prepare us for their death. They can be a valuable source of guidance and encouragement.

Precognitive dreams, visitation dreams, and telepathy dreams show us existence beyond the physical body. It is one thing to believe that there is an afterlife; it is another to taste the experience. People who have had near death experiences report a sense of peace, comfort and bliss, absence of pain, and a feeling of compassionate love on the "other side."[2] People who experience dream visitations from deceased loved ones report similar feelings.

Through dreamstates, we can aid one another and communicate in ways beyond the reach of our (sometimes limited) conscious mind and brain. People who are aware of these "psi" dreams experience the profound realization that there is much more to us than we can see, touch, taste, feel, and hear with our physical senses.

Perhaps this chapter may give you hope and inspiration. It describes some of the intuitive dreams I have had, and how they enabled me to help others, to relieve fears, and to be prepared for events that would have otherwise been shocking to my conscious mind. I will present some exercises anyone can use to strengthen their ability to connect with other people telepathically and to develop the kind of mental rapport that facilitates inner level communication.

What Are Dreams?

This may seem like an obvious question; yet, people have different perspectives of the dream experience. In my School of Metaphysics education, I have learned that dreams occur in the subconscious mind. When we go to sleep at night, we withdraw attention and life force from the conscious mind, physical body, and physical senses, and turn our awareness inward to experience the subconscious mind or soul. We call this the "inner self."

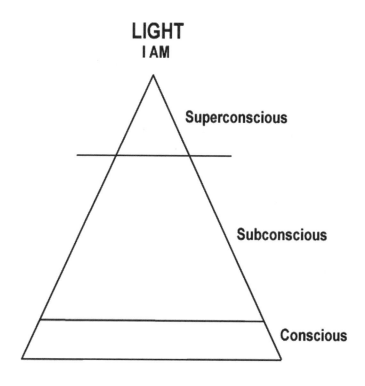

LIGHT
I AM

Superconscious

Subconscious

Conscious

*Diagram of the Mind
and Levels of Consciousness*[3]

3

The experience of going to sleep and withdrawing attention from the body and conscious mind is very similar to the process of death. The difference is that we return from sleep; we gradually (or suddenly, in the case of being startled awake by a noise or alarm clock) transfer awareness to the conscious mind and physical senses. In death the withdrawal is complete; there is no return of attention to the physical senses and body, no life force that animates the body.

Multi-Dimensional Experience

I understand dreams to be multi-dimensional. Some dreams are purely symbolic. Others have the additional significance of being direct experiences in subconscious mind. These are the dreams in which we are visited by those who have withdrawn (died) from physical existence. Some are telepathic messages from other people. There are also precognitive dreams that alert us to probable future events, preparing us to respond to crises or "unexpected" events with greater peace and equanimity.

How do we know when a dream is purely symbolic and when it is one of these direct intuitive happenings? The best answer I can give is, "experience." By paying attention to dreams on a daily basis and keeping a dream journal, we have a record of the precognitions (dreaming of an event which later happens). We become aware of our dreaming. Most people report precognitive, telepathic, and visitation dreams as feeling very "real." The people, places, and events match what occurs in the outer, waking life. Most people awaken from these dreams with the sense that something profound occurred, even when they may not remember all the details.

Intuition can be defined as "inner teaching" or the direct grasp of truth. When we view something intellectually we think about it, we view it as being apart from ourselves. Intuition comes from direct experience. All five senses can be involved, collectively receiving and sensing as a "knowing." Some intuitive experiences are clear and calm. People may have a sense of objectivity, simply observing the occurrence with a sense of knowing. Many people who have had near death experiences describe them this way. They see their body below, without feeling any physical pain, wondering why the other people around the body seem so upset.

Some intuitive or psychic perceptions are more emotional. Oftentimes the emotional state occurs when the perceiver's mind is not still. The experience may be triggering old memories or unresolved issues in the dreamer. This might color the direct perception of truth we call intuition. When we awaken from a dream with anxiety, fear, or foreboding, it may be symbolic, or we may be absorbing emotions and "shock" from other people.

Learning when a dream is a direct perception and when it is symbolic is often a product of experience. We may not know until after-the-fact that our clairvoyance was, indeed, forecasting the future. Many people report that dreams of precognition and direct contact (such as telepathy or visitations from the deceased) are experienced with peace, clarity, and insight when the ones with whom they are connecting "on the other side" are at peace.

Precognitive Dreams

Precognition means to know something in advance. The subconscious mind has an omniscient perspective; thus, it can perceive probable future events. Dreams can give us a peek into these probabilities. The future is probable, not predestined, since we have free will. This means that we can cause change. Thoughts we think today produce our future. With practice, we can learn to perceive this forward-extending stream of consciousness.

Some precognitive dreams can prepare us for a future that might be shocking to the conscious mind. This is why people may dream of disasters before they occur. Some people feel responsible, thinking that they should do something to avert the event before it happens. Although there are times when we can change the future, there are other times when it is not in our hands to make the change. It is up to the other people involved.

Why, then, do we dream of events over which we have no control? We have these dreams because we do have control of our attitudes and state of mind. The precognitive dreams can help us be prepared.

One of the most famous precognitive dreams is the one President Lincoln had shortly before his assassination. He dreamed of seeing a coffin in the East Room surrounded by soldiers who were acting as guards. When he asked, "Who is dead in the White House?" one of the soldiers answered, "The President. He was killed by an assassin." Did the dream enable him to change the event? No. However, it may have helped him and those to whom he reported it.

Not all precognitive dreams concern disasters or crises. Sometimes they are dreams of mundane events. Several years ago I had such a dream:

> *I dream that I go upstairs and D*** is in the bedroom changing the diaper of his baby boy. The baby is wearing a light blue "onesie."*

I had this dream when some friends of mine were expecting a baby. They did not know the gender of the baby. D*** is the father. The morning after I had the dream, I told B***, the expectant mother, about it. She laughed, not knowing if it was purely symbolic or something more.

As it turned out, the baby was a boy. Of course, there is a 50% chance with a dream like that of being proved correct! The profound experience for me, however, was that when the baby was a month old, I experienced the exact scene that was in the dream. I was in the same building, walked upstairs to the room in my dream, and saw D*** bending over the table changing the baby's diaper. The baby was wearing the blue onesie in the dream. Only after I had this experience did I know that the dream was precognitive.

Why did I have this dream? I don't believe it was for the benefit of the parents. Knowing the gender of the expected baby wasn't necessary to prepare the parents or me. They were ready to welcome a child of either gender and did not want to know ahead of time whether the baby would be a boy or a girl.

For me, the dream was significant because it was the first of a series of precognitive dreams. Those dreams were instrumental in helping me to help my husband who was very sick. This seemingly innocuous dream was a beginning step for me to recognize when a dream was precognitive. Prior to this time, I had had other precognitive dreams that I had doubted. This experience helped me to build trust in my own intuitive process.

Changing the Future

What happens when we dream of a future event that we *can* change? Should we? Does the dreamer have a responsibility to make a different future? I don't think there is a universal answer to this question. Making these choices is part of our own process of learning.

Over fifteen years ago I was married to a man who had juvenile diabetes. Diabetes is a disease with serious complications. John, my late husband, went from being quite active and seemingly healthy to developing problems with his vision, kidneys, and heart. He eventually became blind, went on dialysis, and died while waiting for a kidney transplant.

During the time of his progressively failing health, John and I were faced with many decisions concerning his health care. Both of us were students of the School of Metaphysics, practicing spiritual healing, visualization, dreamwork, and intuitive development. John experimented with both allopathic and alternative treatments. At times it seemed as if his body and mind were on a roller coaster; one day he was active and feeling well, another day he was sick, at other times had to be rushed to the emergency room because of a medical crisis.

John and I had a close friendship and very deep love for one another. Before his health was so precarious, we practiced connecting with each other through intuition. For the first few years of our marriage, we were living in different cities and we made "dream dates." We planned to meet in our dreams at a particular location, recorded our results in a dream journal, and then compared notes the next day. Sometimes we were successful in the rendezvous and other times the results were not so clear.

We also intentionally projected thoughts and images to each other while awake. Our telepathic connection became very strong. We frequently knew when the other one was going to call. Sometimes I wanted to contact John but didn't know where he was (he was working as a substitute teacher at the time and was in a different place of work each day). This was in the days before we had cell phones, and there was not always a phone available to make or receive a phone call. So I would send a telepathic message for him to call, and soon he would.

This telepathic rapport became a lifesaver. On two occasions I had clear dreams that enabled me to help John when he needed it.

The first time, I was in Windyville, Missouri and he was in Springfield, 50 miles away.

I dream that John is having a low blood sugar reaction and can't wake up.

That was the dream. Simple, clear, and direct. John was insulin dependent. Insulin is a drug that lowers blood sugar, prescribed for diabetics whose blood sugar becomes dangerously high. Too much insulin can induce a coma and result in death. The hypoglycemic reaction produces a state of grogginess, confusion, inability to think or reason. Once the blood sugar becomes too low, the person is completely unable to respond.

When I awoke, I strongly believed that this dream was not symbolic. I perceived that John was about to slip into a hypoglycemic coma and that he needed help. I didn't know if he was alone or if there was someone else in the house where he was sleeping. I also didn't know if there was still time for him to hear me or if I needed someone else to rescue him.

I immediately telephoned John. The phone rang and rang. No answer. I was scared that he would not be able to answer the phone, so I sent a very strong telepathic message, picturing John in my mind and mentally calling his name with the command to "Wake up and answer the phone!" I called again and let the phone ring for a long time. John finally picked it up and said, "Hello," in a groggy voice. I could tell that he was, indeed, experiencing insulin shock. I asked him to test his blood sugar while I kept him on the phone. He did not understand what I was asking him and did not do the test. I couldn't tell if he was responding to my instructions to drink some orange juice to raise his blood sugar. I was able to keep him on the phone so that he would stay awake, which was important so that he wouldn't slip into a coma.

Using a different phone, I called a friend of his who lived close by and asked if she could go over and help him. Like an angel, she responded immediately, tested his blood sugar and was able to give him what he needed to raise it so that he could return to reasoning consciousness. She brought him to her home to keep an eye on him until we knew that he would be okay.

This dream, though very brief, alerted me to John's condition even though we were both asleep at the time and in two different cities. I am very grateful that I was aware of the dream, that I trusted it and responded, and in so doing was able to help my husband, with the assistance of our generous friend.

About a year later I had another extraordinary dream. By this time, John's kidneys had failed and he was on dialysis. He had become completely blind. Losing his eyesight was a tremendous blow to John. He loved being independent, active, and creative. One of the biggest challenges for him was losing the freedom of being able to drive. Nonetheless, he tried to maintain a positive attitude and insisted on keeping his job as a telemarketer even though he could have received 100% disability and stayed home.

John had recurring problems with infection once he went on dialysis. The dialysis patient has a plastic tube called a graft surgically inserted under the skin, connecting an artery to a vein to provide access to the dialysis machine. John had had several surgeries to replace the grafts in his arm, as they often became infected. For the most part, he kept a good attitude about the increasing numbers of surgeries and hospitalizations, although he hated being incapacitated. I had the second dream when John was out of work recuperating from one of these surgeries.

This dream was also very brief, only a fragment. John and I were at home.

*I dream that John has died. There is a great feeling
of exhilaration, and deep peace. When I awaken, I lie
there in bed, holding the echo of the dream as long as I
can. There is such a feeling of peace, of lightness, as if
I am surrounded by love and filled with a deep light that
permeates my whole being.*

When I awoke, I was startled, because I thought that this had
actually happened. It seemed odd to me that I wasn't scared
or panicked or anxious or sad. The feeling in the dream was
wonderful; I felt a wave of peace and exhilaration wash over me.
I wanted to share it with John who was lying in bed next to me,
sleeping, and alive. I wondered if I should tell him about the
dream, as I didn't want to alarm him. At the same time, it felt so
real I thought I owed it to him to let him know.

When I told John about the dream, I wondered if he would
be anxious or worried. He wasn't; he just listened. Maybe I told
him too soon after he awoke and he wasn't fully conscious, or
maybe he was simply accepting it.

I left that morning to go to work and he stayed home, still
recovering from the surgery from the removal of the infected
graft. After being at work for a couple of hours, I was in the
middle of a project and I felt an incredibly strong urge to call
John. When I called he sounded panicky. He was just about to
call me.

"Laurel," he said, "I need your help. There's something
dripping in the kitchen and I don't know what it is. I think I
might be bleeding." I thought that he might just be anxious,
but I dropped what I was doing to go see. Since he was blind, he
could not see for himself what was happening.

When I arrived home and walked in the door, John said to
me, "Laurel, don't panic, there's a lot of blood in here." His voice
sounded emotion-less, like he was holding on to every shred
of sanity he could muster. When I walked into the kitchen, I
saw John standing at the sink, holding his arm over the sink.
There was blood spurting from the place in his arm where they
removed the graft. There was blood everywhere: in the sink, on
the floor. There was about a quarter inch of sticky blood all over
the kitchen floor. John's footprints on the floor showed where

he had tracked blood walking from the sink to the phone on the counter. John had the phone in his hand; it was caked with blood. This was unlike anything I had seen, even in movies.

I have told the rest of this story in a book I wrote called **Karmic Healing**.[4] The part I want to recount here concerns the significance of the dream I had that morning. That day John was in emergency rooms in two different hospitals. He was rushed by ambulance to a hospital in Lebanon, Missouri, transferred by ambulance to the dialysis center there, and then later in the day was rushed again by ambulance to a different hospital in Springfield, Missouri.

All day long John and I were faced with decisions about how to respond to this artery that kept spurting blood. The doctors kept thinking they had it under control, and then it started bleeding again. John had several transfusions that day and almost died several times. He finally went into emergency surgery around midnight.

I called a friend and mentor of mine at midnight, as soon as John was taken into surgery. I told her about the dream I had had. She asked me if I had contacted John's mother who lived in Arizona. In my own reaction to taking care of John, following the ambulance, trying to decide when and if surgery was needed, it hadn't even occurred to me to call her. It was late, I didn't want to disturb her; yet, the dream stimulated me to call her anyway. Although I did not want to admit it, I thought that it could well be precognitive.

My mother-in-law is a very gracious woman whose strong religious life includes prayer. When I woke her up with this news, she was concerned and wanted to know if she should fly to Missouri. I didn't know what to tell her; I let her know about the dream and also told her that I thought the surgeon was a good one. She immediately got on the phone to contact all of John's brothers and sisters, his aunts and uncle, and her friends. She asked them all to pray for him.

The surgery was effective. John lived.

Was this a precognitive dream? Who is to say? John almost died several times that day. The dream gave me a sense of calm that enabled me to deal with the repeated crises. It also motivated me to call my mentor, who suggested I call John's mother, who then asked all of her family and friends to pray for John. Perhaps their prayers caused his recovery. Some skeptics might doubt this, saying that the surgery could have worked without their prayers. The truth is, we don't know if we changed the course of events. I do know that the dream gave me guidance, insight, and a peek into the peace of mind that comes with death.

The Peace of Death

I had another dream that had a similar feeling. This one occurred about a year after John died. The complications of diabetes finally took their toll, and John withdrew from the physical (died) on September 10, 2000. A year later, on September 11, 2001, I decided that I was going to take a day off of work and spend it quietly by myself to complete a year of mourning.

I was driving to the closest town when I heard the news on the radio. "The second tower has been hit!" The announcer in an alarmed voice was reporting the second attack on the World Trade Center in New York City. I spent the rest of that day in a kind of stupor. Every place I went, people looked stricken, their faces ashen, their eyes glazed over. No one could believe what had happened.

I grew up just outside of New York City and have friends who live there. John's oldest sister and her son live in Manhattan. I tried to call them to see if they were okay, but none of the phone lines were connecting. Everything seemed very surreal and it was impossible to make any physical connection with anyone I knew in New York.

That night, I had the following dream:

I dream that John is in New York, helping the people who died in the World Trade Center. I am so happy to see him. I ask him, "Are they okay?" He smiles this beautiful smile, full of light, and radiates love. "Yes!" he says. "They're fine! Once they are out, they're fine!" I know he means that once they are out of the body they are fine, with no pain because they are released from the bodily prison. I can feel the peace and exhilaration.

I woke up feeling relieved, peaceful, and happy. I knew that when John was alive he was always helping other people, so it made sense that he was still helping people on the other side. I also knew that this was a visitation, an actual communication from him. It helped me to be at peace and to be a calming presence for other people I knew who were extremely grief-stricken and outraged at what had occurred. It also helped me to ease my grief at John's passing, because in the dream he could see, he was vibrant, and he was at his best, helping other people.

Visitations

This dream is called a visitation. It is fairly common for people who have died to come to their loved ones in a dream, to "visit" in the inner levels of the subconscious mind. Most people experience visitation dreams as comforting and reassuring.

When I was fifteen years old my father died. I missed him terribly and did not understand his death. I was taught that when you are dead, you cease to exist. I was not raised to believe in an afterlife, so I felt abandoned and alone when he died.

When my husband died, there were resonances with my father's death. Both men were very important to me. I loved them deeply and they loved and accepted me. Both were very nurturing, affectionate, friendly, and humorous. They helped me to bring out those qualities in myself. When they died, it was difficult for me to be lighthearted without their stimulus.

Both deaths occurred after a period of illness. My father had cancer and in the last year or two of his life he was so drugged with pain medications that his consciousness was in and out.

No one knew when he would die, and he lived far longer than any of the doctors expected. I never got to say goodbye, as he died when I was away on a summer vacation.

My husband's health was up and down. None of the doctors ever said how long John had to live; they were expecting that he would have a kidney transplant so no one spoke of him as being terminally ill. In some ways his death came as a surprise. One of the nurses at the dialysis center said, when I told her that he died, "But he was doing so well!" I never had a chance to say goodbye to him either.

The great difference when my husband died was that I had a much deeper understanding of what happens after death. I had studied and practiced metaphysics and spiritual disciplines such as meditation, dream interpretation, lucid dreaming, and consciously entering the inner levels of consciousness. I had practiced telepathy with John and our intuitive connection was strong.

So I believed that John would come to me in my dreams after he died. I was very disappointed when that didn't happen right away, or at least I was not aware of it happening. John was my best friend and I really missed him. I just wanted to talk to him, to say goodbye, to let him know that I loved him and hear him tell me that he loved me.

For the first couple of weeks after his death I had difficulty sleeping and wanted to sleep so that John could visit me in my dreams! About a month after his death, when I still had not had a visitation dream, I decided that I would clearly ask John to come to me. Before going to bed, I wrote a long letter to him in my journal. I meditated. Then I wrote in my dream journal, "John, please come to me in my dreams."

That night I had the following dream:

*I am in a large auditorium. There is a ceremony on stage, like a graduation ceremony. I see John on the stage, wearing a baseball cap. I wave to him but I am not sure if he sees me. Later, someone brings me my **Bible** which has been left on the stage. I open it and a piece of paper flutters out.*

On it, there is a heart, drawn in John's handwriting. I cry, because I know it is him saying, "I love you."

This dream was bittersweet. When I awoke, I knew that it was a visitation. I also knew that the reason John had not come to me in my dreams before this was that he was still getting used to his body in the inner levels. He was just "graduating" to his new stage of life after death. He couldn't talk yet and could not write. He could gesture and communicate in pictures.

I cherished this dream, because the feeling was very loving and peaceful. It helped me to respect where John was in his process of assimilation, and to be patient, waiting for him to be "born again" in the inner levels and develop greater facility using his new body.

The patience paid off. Soon after this, I had several waking visitations from John. The first occurred three months after he died. My mother, who had been healthy and active at the age of 79, playing tennis every morning and riding her bicycle every day, suddenly had a massive stroke. It was December. In Missouri we were in the midst of a huge ice storm. I had to rush home to pack so that I could fly to Florida where she was in the hospital.

I was upset, and scared. I didn't want to speed on the country roads which were covered in ice; at the same time I knew that I had to move quickly to drive to the airport so I could catch the first flight out. I felt completely alone, and I was really missing John, for I knew that if he were there he would comfort me and help me to relax.

When I arrived home, I was about to walk in the front door when the wind chimes outside the front door started to move. Prior to this the air had been completely still, with no wind. The wind picked up the chimes when I walked toward them. I suddenly felt John's presence, his strong and comforting love, as if he were hugging me from behind. I heard him, as if he were whispering in my ear, "I'm with you. I'm here."

I started to cry, not out of sadness, but from relief. John had loved those wind chimes, which sounded like rich temple bells. Because he was blind the last two years of his life, sounds were very meaningful to him. Those chimes had been a wedding present and they symbolized love to both of us. His steadying presence helped me to pack, to drive to the airport, and to be centered. I knew that he was with me. It was not just a memory of him; he was there.

A few weeks later, John came to me again. My friend S***'s mother was in the hospital for a surgery to have her leg amputated. Her mother was also a diabetic who had become a dialysis patient and had lost her eyesight. She and John had become friends, sharing stories of their experiences with the illness. John had given her some advice about resources he'd discovered. After John died, I gave her some of the devices John had for blind people (talking clocks, talking blood sugar meters, a talking scale.)

*I woke up, suddenly. It felt as if John were shaking me awake. He told me that S***'s mother died.* I noted the time, 5:15 a.m. I immediately projected thoughts of love and understanding to her, and told her to reach out to people she knew who would help her cross over. I sent a mental message to John, thanking him and asking him to guide her. I heard him laugh in his good-natured way, as if I was being a know-it-all when he was the one giving the guidance. I also sent a projection of love and understanding to S*** and her sisters, and prayed for them all. I knew that they were facing difficult times.

Later that morning, we received a call from S*** telling us her mother had died at 5:15 a.m.

How Intuitive Dreaming Can Help Us

Precognitive dreams and visitation dreams can help alleviate fear because the subconscious mind is omniscient and objective. The subconscious mind or soul views life from the perspective of learning. It does not judge experience as good or bad, pleasurable or painful, happy or sad. It accepts. It sees what is.

Learning to receive from the subconscious mind can help us to create a similar kind of objective, compassionate state of mind. Remembering and experiencing these dreams gives us a taste of our Real Self, the self that exists beyond the limitations of physical time, physical senses, and the accompanying pain or judgment.

Exercises to Strengthen Telepathic Rapport

Strengthening your telepathic rapport with people while they are alive helps to build a familiar connection with them. When they die, it can then be easier to communicate with them in the dream state.

You may enjoy developing this affinity with mind exercises. Here are a few to get you started.

1. ESP card projection

Practice telepathy with a partner by projecting images to one another, taking turns with one person being the sender and one being the receiver. You might start with a deck of children's flash cards that have simple images of objects like animals, trees, or houses. Or use brightly colored squares of construction paper, projecting the colors.

You can also print out ESP cards developed in the 1930's by Karl Zener and J.B. Rhine from websites such as psychicscience. org. These cards feature black geometric symbols on a white background. Twenty cards is a good number to use in the beginning.

With your friend, choose one person to send and one to receive. The receiver sits quietly, with a piece of paper and a pen. Breathe deeply several times to clear the mind. The sender also breathes deeply. Then, one at a time, the sender looks at the card, seeing the image (or color, or shape), "feeling" it, and saying it in his mind. (For example, if projecting the flash card images, the sender says clearly in his mind, "House!" while visualizing the picture shown on the card.) The sender can feel the image radiate out from his solar plexus area or image throwing it like a ball to the receiver.

The receiver writes down the first image (or color, or shape) she receives. She needs to practice trusting herself. Usually it is best to capture the first impression without second-guessing it. She may feel it, or see it, or hear it, or smell it, or taste it. It might be received as a "knowing." After going through all 20 cards, compare notes and then switch so that the sender is now the receiver and vice versa.

2. Establish dream dates.

Decide in advance when you want to share a mutual dream. Choose a location, preferably a physical location that is well known and liked by you and your friend or partner. Visualize yourself being at that place together before you go to sleep. Agree upon what you will do there in your dream. (sit by a fire, eat dinner together, hold hands, etc.) Or you might explore a common concept, like love or gratitude. Form a clear image and expectation of being there and write down whatever you experience in your dream. Share your dreams with each other when you awaken.

3. Thought projection.

Exchange an object that belongs to you with your friend or partner. This should be some object that is infused with your vibration; it could be a piece of jewelry you wear often, an object that is on your desk that you handle often, a favorite item of clothing. The idea is to choose something that has your vibration strongly impressed in it. Also exchange a recent photograph of yourselves with each other. (Select a photo that you like.)

Choose a time to project a thought to your partner, and a different time when he or she will project a thought to you. Do this when you are in different physical locations. When you are projecting the thought, your friend should be in a receptive state, in a place where he can write down what thoughts enter his mind. Before you project, look at your friend's picture and fill your mind with love for him. Hold his object in your hand, close your eyes, and feel his vibration. Then, with eyes open or closed, hold the image of his face in mind and call out to him mentally. Project the desired thought. Picture it and say the words in your mind. Write down what you project. Later, compare notes about what you projected and what he received during this time.

At a different time, switch roles so that you are receiving the thought your friend is projecting to you. You may discover that you are stronger with sending or receiving, or you may find that you are balanced. You may find that certain kinds of thoughts are easier for you to send or receive.

These are just a few of many exercises you can practice to develop telepathy and dream projection. Through my studies at the School of Metaphysics, I have learned valuable principles of thought-form projection, such as always asking permission before projecting healing, and always keeping the other person's best interest in mind. Mind-to-mind connection can be very harmonious.

Why Pay Attention to Dreams?

Messages from Your Soul

"Dreams are faithful interpreters of our own inclinations; but there is an art required to sort and understand them."

— Montaigne, Of Experience

When I was a child I had difficulty falling asleep at night. I can remember being four or five years old, lying in bed, watching the hands of the clock go around. Sometimes I'd creep out of bed and sit on the balcony of my room, looking out at the night sky. Other times, I entertained myself by making up stories or allowing my mind to float.

I used to reach out with my mind to imagine where the universe ended. I could imagine as far as my neighborhood, and beyond the neighborhood to the next suburb where some family friends lived. Then, I could imagine other states which we had visited on vacation. I'd continue to stretch my mind to imagine as far as I could, and even beyond, out into the sky. Eventually I'd drift into sleep.

I also had experiences of synesthesia that came to me as I was lying in bed. The days of the week and the months of the year appeared to me with colors and shapes. They were consistent. Each day had a particular shape (round-ish or rectangle with round corners, or long and skinny in a horizontal shape, or amorphous and wide) and specific colors. The months did also.

Every so often I'd check in to make sure that the days or months were still the same color. Then, as I let my mind float through the days of the week, I'd fall asleep.

I loved it when I could feel myself falling through a kind of tunnel, like going down a slide. If I could stay awake as I went down the slide, I would feel myself slip into a dream. These were my first early experiences with lucidity in the dream state. At some point, I lost the ability to maintain awareness as I crossed into the dreamworld. Gradually, the synesthesia dissolved too.

There was no particular incident (at least that I can remember) that marked the end of these experiences, but it seems to coincide with the time that I entered kindergarten. Entering public school was a shock. I had looked forward to school for what seemed like a long time, ever since my older sister went to kindergarten two years before me. It was not what I was expecting, however. I was a shy, introverted child and did not enjoy being in a classroom full of kids I didn't know. I was often embarrassed and felt out of place. I loved to read, but my teacher told me I should play with the other kids. The challenge was that I didn't know how to initiate being a part of a group so I felt quite alone.

Turning my attention outward to the physical world and trying to fulfill what I believed to be the expectations of my teacher and the "society" of school also meant turning away from my real, genuine, natural Self. The re-discovery of who I am and bringing that inner Self forward has been a lifelong process. Re-establishing a relationship with my dreams has aided me in awakening the Real Self that I learned to suppress so long ago. Becoming more centered in who I AM, has aided me to become more at ease in relationships with other people, the lesson I needed to learn in kindergarten but did not know how.

I love the many ways that dreams can be used for greater Self awareness, peace of mind, developing intuition, and for fulfilling who you are to become this lifetime.

Why Am I Here?
Many people believe that there is some reason for being here on this earth that goes beyond having a good job, making good

money and even having a good family. Some people make choices in the pursuit of the answer to the question, "Why am I here?" while others just contemplate the idea or decide that they will only know after death.

Studies of those who are dying have found that there are universal questions people ask themselves at the end of life. These are not questions about financial security, fame or reputation, or possessions. They are:

1) Did I give and receive love?
2) Did I become all that I could be?
3) Did I leave the world a little bit better?

What if we asked ourselves these questions every day, rather than waiting to be on our deathbed? We could have an enriching life by determining how to give and receive love, to become all we can be, and to leave the world a little bit better.[1]

Try this exercise. Have someone read these words to you, or record them and listen to the directions. Close your eyes and just relax. Direct your attention to the very center of your being, near the pit of your stomach, your solar plexus area. Imagine there a very beautiful light. See it being very brilliant, very pure, and cause it to expand until it fills your whole body and radiates throughout your whole being. See yourself completely surrounded with this light.

Now go back in your memory. Go back to a time, either in the recent past or when you were a young child, any time in your life that you remember being very joyous. Choose an experience where the joy welled up within you, with a wonderful, peaceful feeling, in love with the world and everything and everyone around you. Just let your

mind drift to this time and remember what you were doing and where you were.

Keep this joyous time in your mind and bring your attention gently back. Bring it back to the here and now, to your physical body. Bring it back to the place where you are sitting. Now place your attention on your feet, gradually move your attention up your legs, up your back, all the way up to the crown of your head, so that you are fully centered in the here and now. Take a deep breath and as you inhale, open your eyes.

Did you feel the joy? This could be your natural state. Most people believe that they should experience happiness. However, oftentimes they do not live their lives *being* happy. If you listen to people talk on the bus, or in a restaurant, or at work, you frequently hear them complain about what is wrong. They grumble about their jobs, the weather, current events, the government, their health. It seems that bliss is rare.

That does not seem reasonable. It doesn't make sense to live to be 50, 60, or 100 years old, being joyful on rare occasions while most of the time life is depressing or dull or boring. It seems like we should enjoy life and only be discontent once in awhile.

The guided imagery was designed for you to draw out of yourself the awareness of what brings you joy. You can live with that deep peace every day of your life. It does not cost money, and it is not too difficult to attain. The potential for such fulfillment is with you all the time and comes from your soul or inner self.

Your inner self is the "you" that is eternal, that lasts beyond this physical body. It remains throughout the ups and downs of everyday life. It is steady through emotional upheavals and mood swings. It is always there. You might call it your genuine Self, your Real Self. When you experience joy, it bubbles up from within you, wells up and surrounds you and makes everything and everyone around you happy.

His Holiness the Dalai Lama teaches happiness as an art. In a teaching on "*The Art of Happiness*" at Colgate College in New York, His Holiness said that inner peace, compassion, and truth are necessary for happiness. He implored his audience to "please think more about those inner values." and said, "We pay too much concern to material things and neglect our inner resources."[2]

Night-time dreams are an "inner resource." Dreams come from your soul. Have you ever awakened from a dream with the feeling that something profound had happened? Even if you do not remember the dream, you might emerge from sleep with the sense that something deep and meaningful had just occurred. This sense of meaning can suffuse your everyday life when you listen to the voice of your soul.

When you came into this lifetime, your soul knew why you were here. As you have grown and developed, you have made choices with your conscious mind, the reasoning/thinking capacity. Those conscious choices have either been aligned with your soul, bringing you joy and peace and contentment, or they have diverted you from heeding your soul's urge. When you are off course, the dull depression sets in, when you think, "I don't even know why I'm getting up in the morning."

Through understanding your dreams you can re-discover why you are here and how to fulfill your life's purpose. You dream in the inner levels of your own consciousness. This is your subconscious mind or your soul. Your dreams tell you about you. Every dream you have can tell you about the state of your awareness. That is the purpose of dreams: they communicate to you a message about you. The dreams come from your inner self and can give you insight into your own feelings and attitudes.

When you learn how to interpret your dreams, it is like having an inner guide or teacher who can advise, instruct, or reflect to you what is in your best interest. You build a conscious connection with your inner Self. You become more secure, more content, nourished from within. You learn to hear what your inner self wants and needs.

Your Assignment in Life

Developing a relationship with your inner self can aid you to understand and resolve your karmic lessons as well as drawing out your understanding and talent, or dharma. The dharma is related to one of the three questions people ask at the end of life: did I leave the world a little bit better? That is your gift to offer the world. Everyone has something unique to contribute. Your duty to humanity is to give what you have to make the world a better place. Some people call this your soul's assignment.[3]

That is not the same as your karma. Your karma is what you are here to learn this lifetime. It is a kind of debt you owe to yourself, to better yourself, to grow in character, to develop mentally, emotionally and spiritually. The karma and dharma go hand-in-hand. As you give yourself to aid others, you learn your karmic lessons. In the process of bettering yourself, you leave the world a better place. As I understand it, we are here both to learn the lessons the soul needs to be complete, and to minister to others by sharing what we have already made a part of ourselves.

When you resonated with a joyful experience in the guided imagery, it is likely that you were remembering a time when you were giving from your soul. That enthusiasm is a creative wellspring that bubbles up from within you when you give from a place inside of you that is deep and real.

Knowing your assignment can aid you to experience this deep joy on a regular basis. When you are in school, you complete assignments so that you can learn. They serve a purpose: to apply yourself, to draw out of yourself what you know, to put forth effort, to learn something new.

You can look at this world as being like a schoolroom for us to learn who we are and how to create a meaningful existence. When you are carrying out your soul's assignment, bequeathing your inner gifts, you learn; you fulfill your karma. As you offer your understanding for the benefit of others, you relieve your karma. You fill in the empty places that your soul needs to complete.

Your dreams can tell you about what you have to offer. They can show you about what you need to learn. They can guide you in your soul progression. They can point out when you are learning and when you are shutting off your learning. A common dream for many adults is some version of the following:

I am back in school (high school or college). I am wandering the halls and can't find my classroom. When

I finally find the room, I am panicked because there is a test and I realize I haven't attended the class all semester so I'm not prepared.

I understand this dream to be telling the dreamer that she is aware that there is something she needs to learn in her waking life, some life lesson, that she is not getting. Maybe she needs to be more outspoken and there are waking experiences that are "testing" her, like friends who talk louder than she or a boss who doesn't listen. But rather than doing something about it, she just says to herself, "Yeah, there must be something for me to learn because this keeps happening to me."

When the dreamer practices what she needs to learn, such as having the courage to say what is on her mind or to interrupt the incessant talker, the dream changes. She will pass the test, or maybe even teach the class!

> *The symbols are universal and the message is personal.*

The Personal and the Universal

As I understand it, the symbols are universal and the message is personal. Only the dreamer can determine how a particular dream applies to his or her life. When you interpret your own dreams, it is like having a counselor who sits on the edge of your bed upon awakening to say, "Hey, this is what's going on with you and this is what you can do about it." That seems comforting, to know that you can have a relationship every day with your inner self.

Dreams are timeless. We can learn from them as soon as we remember them, and we can derive meaning from them years later, when we have a different perspective. I had the following dream when I was in college. At the time, I did not know how to interpret dreams so I just wrote it in my journal:

I am in a parking garage. I am being chased by someone or a group of people who are menacing, and I feel panicked. Then I realize I can fly, but I keep running into the walls of the parking garage. Then, suddenly, in the dream, I realized that if I picture the sky above the garage, and concentrate on filling my mind with the image of the sky, I can emerge from the garage. It works! I picture the sky, and then I am out of the garage!

I found this dream recently, when I was looking through my old journals to research house dreams for the *"That Recurring Dream House"* presentation in this book. The other journal entries showed me that I had this dream when I was finally resolving some troubling emotional issues from my early teenage years. I was seeing a counselor who encouraged me to record my dreams and act them out. She taught me how to use Gestalt methods to express emotions that I had buried. The counseling was liberating. I was discovering that the emotional paralysis that had plagued me since I was twelve years old was of my own making, and I could break free of the restrictions by visualizing myself in new ways.

From my current vantage point, I understand that the dream reflected this new awakening. I interpret the sky as superconscious mind, above the entrapments and limitations of the physical existence. Just knowing there is a sky beyond the garage or warehouse aids me to reach for it ... and gives me hope and faith that enables me to break free of whatever is restricting me. It reminds me of one of my favorite quotes, from a poem by Robert Browning, "A man's reach must exceed his grasp, or what's a heaven for?"

I found this dream in my journal more than thirty years after I recorded it, and yet, the message still applies to my life. This is one benefit of keeping a dream journal — it gives us a record of our soul growth and aids in understanding cycles of learning. When people continue to learn, they are bright and youthful at any age!

The School of Metaphysics publishes an ebook called **Mechanics of Dreams** by Dr. Jerry Rothermel. Dr. Rothermel wrote in that book that you can tell a person who remembers his dreams because he has a light in his eyes. That stimulated me to look for it, and I found it to be true. You can also tell when people have forgotten or blocked their dreams because their eyes are dull. The light has gone out.

People who have a connection with their inner Self have luminous eyes, and people who do not have that affinity show it with lackluster eyes. You can see it in yourself when you look in the mirror. Children, especially young children, radiate that light. Most children remember their dreams. They wake up telling you about their dreams even if they do not know what they mean.

Remembering your dreams is satisfying because they are always truthful. Your inner Self can only relate truth. Your conscious mind is not always like that. It can lie to you. Your conscious mind can rationalize. The ego-driven "you" can make choices that do not seem to be in the best interest of your soul. Think about people who become involved in relationships that are destructive. Or those who make "get rich quick" business decisions that crash. Some people make choices based on what "feels good" without thinking ahead about their consequences.

Feelings, because they are temporary, are not always an accurate gauge for making correct choices. Sometimes what feels good now feels bad in an hour. A piece of pie may look appetizing and taste sweet, but it may feel unpleasant as it digests if you have already eaten too much sugar. Spending money on an indulgence might feel good today and not so good tomorrow when you discover your checkbook is overdrawn. Emotions fluctuate so if you make decisions based on those feelings, you are at the whim of temporary moods. That can be a tough way to live. It wears you out after awhile.

If you respond to an inner "feeling" such as kindness or compassion or patience or tolerance, then doing what "feels good" can work. This inner sense of conscience comes from knowing what is permanent. It is purposeful.

31

Most people want security. When the economy is uncertain, when relationships are in flux, when weather disasters loom, it seems like nothing endures. Dreams can aid us to discover lasting satisfaction by pointing the way to self-understanding. I think that most people would agree that even difficult experiences can be rewarding when we grow through them — becoming a better person or developing our character in some way. Our nighttime dreams can give us feedback regarding how we have learned such lessons in our waking state.

It is nourishing to listen to the wisdom that resides within you. Your inner Self embraces and loves what causes inner growth. It is only the habitual, physical self that fights change, trying to hang on to things that are temporary. When you learn how to interpret your dreams, you can let go of limitations and make conscious choices that say "Yes!" to your inner self. With daily practice, it becomes natural to keep that kind of awareness alive in yourself every day.

The secret is to know how to interpret the messages your dreams give you. As you learn to understand your dreams and apply those messages to your life, you will have resolution. You will live well and be able to rest your head on the pillow when you go to sleep at night.

When everyone on the planet knows how to interpret dreams, the consciousness of the universe will be raised! We will get along much better with one another, for as we know ourselves, we have greater peace of mind. When our fears are relieved (dream interpretation can do this), we trust each other more completely. A simple thing like remembering and interpreting dreams has profound consequences for ourselves, our lives, our relationships, and our world.

Friends, Strangers, Soul Mates and Other Dream Characters

I keep having these dreams about this guy I know at school. He looks at me and winks. Yet, when I am awake, he hardly notices me. Why do I keep dreaming about him?

I was doing a radio interview, interpreting dreams on the air, when a junior high school girl called in with this dream. She was hoping that the dream meant that her "dreamboat" liked her. What does it mean when people appear in our dreams? Sometimes they are strangers. Sometimes we dream of people we knew years ago but haven't seen for decades. Some dreams feature characters we have only seen in movies, or read about in books. Some people have frequent dreams of people they see every day.

Who are these dream characters? Are they symbols? Actual visitations with those people? Or are they precognitions of future events?

In my thirty years experience with dreams, as a student and as a teacher, I have learned that dreams can be understood as multi-dimensional. I would say that people in dreams can be all of these: symbols, visitations, and precognitions. All dreams can be interpreted symbolically, and some dreams may also be actual inner level experiences. Understanding the people in our dreams helps us to understand ourselves.

In waking life, some people have a fragmented kind of existence. Have you ever asked a friend about a decision and he answers, "A part of me wants to take the job, but another part of me is satisfied staying with my current job." Or you may think, "A part of me likes to be by myself and a part of me wonders what I'm missing when other people are in a group." What are these "parts"? One way to understand them is as aspects, or qualities of the self.

For example, one person may be organized, thoughtful, kind, stubborn, intelligent, funny, responsible, impatient, hurried ... get the picture? We have many different qualities that make up who we are.

Sometimes we recognize the different "parts" of the self. Sometimes we may not know ourselves very well. Dreams can aid us to become aware of all of the aspects of the self. The more we can integrate the many aspects of ourselves into a unified whole, the more we experience ourselves as having integrity and peace of mind.

Many people see themselves differently from the way other people see them. Just recently I was listening to a woman who was upset because she seemed "disconnected" from the people she works with. When I asked her how she would describe herself, she said, "loving, compassionate, and friendly." Yet, some of her co-workers described her as aloof and disinterested. Clearly, she was not aware of how she comes across. Although she thinks of herself as loving, she has difficulty expressing emotional warmth so other people don't feel her love. This is in large part why she feels "disconnected." She is out of touch with her own emotions, which then expresses in her relationships with people.

Getting to know yourself can be an enjoyable prospect. A useful exercise is to describe yourself by writing down all of the qualities you identify as being "you." Then, ask other people how they see you. Find out if your image of yourself is consistent with the way other people relate to you. You might discover that different people see you in different ways. Is this a function of their perception, or are you a different person in different situations?

You may find that at your job you are responsible, efficient and organized, and when you are with your kids you are playful, optimistic, and relaxed. Maybe you don't bring the playfulness and optimism into your workplace. So if you were to ask a co-worker how he sees you, he might describe you as responsible and efficient, but would be surprised to hear you say that you are playful and optimistic.

Dreams are a reflection of the thoughts and attitudes we have when awake. The people in dreams can be understood as aspects of the self. So if I dream of my older sister, she symbolizes some quality that is in me. The dreamer is the ultimate authority on his or her dream, so only the dreamer can determine what aspect the dream-person symbolizes.

I see my older sister as being organized and efficient. In fact, she is known to say, "Organization is my middle name." When I dream about her, she symbolizes the quality in me of organization and efficiency. I view my younger sister as being very curious and adventuresome. When I dream of her, she symbolizes those qualities in myself. My younger sister is a more frequent character in my dreams, which makes sense since I identify myself as curious and do not view myself being as structured as my older sister.

Although they are both my sisters, they are two very different people, so they symbolize different aspects of myself in my dreams. This is the first layer of interpreting what people signify in dreams: identify the quality you see in them.

I have found in teaching people to interpret dreams, sometimes they have difficulty identifying the quality that another person symbolizes. They think of other people in terms of their relationship with them. They think about whether they like or dislike the person, if they spend time together, what activities they share. For example, one of my students has frequent dreams with her friend K**. When I asked her what K** symbolizes, she said, "Well, we are friends, so she symbolizes friendship." I asked her what kind of person she sees K** to be, and after giving it some thought, she said, "She always accepts me as I am. She is non-judgmental and she is always encouraging me to keep on going, even when I feel like giving up."

Her friend K**, then, in her own estimation, represents these qualities of acceptance, non-judgmentalism, and encouragement. When K** appears in her dream, it is telling her something about that quality in herself.

(Note: My student A** gave her permission to use this dream and its application in this chapter.)

> *K** and I are out on a street corner with a sign up that lets others know that we can help them. The sign changes for them. One of the ladies who is our age sees the sign as she's going down the hill and then turns back around when she gets to the bottom of the hill.*

> *K** and I pack up and I wonder if the sign has made a difference to others. We then go to where our stuff is (bags, belongings, valuables) and the lady walks up to us. She saw the sign and wants treatment. We sit her down in a chair and K** begins treating her ears, which treats her whole body. She has water coming from her ears dripping down onto her body. I watch as K** treats.*

> *When we are done, the lady thanks us and walks away. I wonder who else's lives we have changed that we won't know about.*

> *Soon the lady comes back with a friend. I wonder if she needs treatment, too. Then I find out why they are there. They want to rob us of our valuables. K** seems okay with it; however, I am not (inwardly) okay. However, I pretend that I am and go to my purse to give it to them. I know that I have a knife in there, on the top, and can quickly access it. I am glad that I have done that by setting my knife up that way. I access it quickly and, with not much effort, kill both girls.*

This is how she interpreted the dream:

"My friend K** symbolizes the aspect of myself that is accepting, encouraging, and unconditionally loving. This aspect of myself has a healing influence. It makes a difference in many other aspects of myself when I am accepting and encouraging. It aids me to hear the truth in my experiences.

The unknown woman who is being treated is an aspect of myself that steals from my own sense of value. This is the aspect of myself that feels unloved, unwanted, and rejected. I am not okay anymore with stealing from myself in this way, and I am beginning to see that I am more valuable than that. Killing the woman and friend who are about to steal from K** and me symbolizes me changing this aspect of myself."

A** had this dream on the evening of her 33rd birthday. She is at a point in her life of trying to understand love, how to be unconditional in giving love to others, and to receive the love that others have for her. She is a woman who enjoys receiving attention from others but oftentimes has difficulty believing that people love her. On the day she had the dream, she had plans with a friend who was driving from another city to take her out to dinner at a special buffet, and then to go to a concert with her friend K** who was also driving from another city.

Several hours before the dinner date, A** received a call from the friend who was traveling. She was stuck in traffic, did not know what was going on with the roads, but thought she would be there soon. A few hours later, A** received another call from the friend, who was still stuck in traffic. Apparently there had been such a severe wreck that the highway was closed and the traffic was at a complete standstill. Then A** learned from her friend K** that her car had broken down and she also would not be able to make it in time for the concert. So A**, very disappointed, decided to go out to dinner and to the concert by herself. As she was driving to the restaurant, she felt very lonely, wondering why, of all days, this had happened on her birthday. Not just one, but both friends, had had unavoidable problems that kept them from being with her to celebrate.

"This always happens to me," she thought. Suddenly, she heard her thoughts of self-pity and rejection and decided that she didn't have to think these old, habitual thoughts. Neither friend had intentionally abandoned her. The highway wreck was not her friend's fault, and she knew that this person left extremely early, with plenty of time to spare. The highway was closed, and there was nothing she could do about it. Nor had her friend K** planned for the car breakdown. A** had to admit that both of the friends loved her, and their inability to make it to her birthday plans had nothing to do with their lack of love.

In that moment, she changed the old pattern of feeling unloved, rejected, and unwanted. She ended up enjoying her birthday, being friendly with the people at the restaurant and making a new friend with the person sitting next to her at the concert. As she went to bed, she reviewed her day and realized that she has people in her life who do love her. With these thoughts in her mind, she had the dream. A** saw the dream as an affirmation that her effort to change the old, limited thought patterns was, indeed, making a difference in her consciousness, and bringing healing to herself.

What does it mean when we have dreams with lots of strangers? Simply, there are many unknown aspects of ourselves. The dreams bring to our attention the fact that there is much more to us than we recognize. One woman I know found that when she first started recording her dreams she often had crowds of strangers. She would be in rooms full of people, none of whom were familiar, or she knew only one person in the room. Over time, by recording her dreams, she was becoming more familiar with different aspects of herself. She began to have more friends and people known to her as dream characters.

What about the person who recurs in our dreams? Our dreams are telling us that this is an important aspect; it is something to which we are giving a lot of attention in our waking state. For example, my student A** has known K** for a while, but only recently had had a series of dreams in which the dream character K** appears. This is significant, because lately A** had been giving a lot of attention to self-acceptance. This is why the person who, in her mind, symbolizes acceptance, is in her psyche at night.

The Conglomerate Character

Some people have a dream character who, in the dream, is one person, but upon awakening, the dreamer identifies that person as a conglomerate of several people he or she has known who all symbolize the same quality.

For example, before I became a student of metaphysics, I had a series of dreams in which there was a dark-haired woman. Upon awakening, I realized this person was a combination of a girl I had known in junior high school, a friend from college, and another friend who was at a summer program I attended. All three women exhibited a similar quality: being very headstrong, self-centered, and assertive. At times I also viewed these women as being selfish.

At that time in my life, I saw myself as fairly passive and indecisive. I would never have described myself as headstrong and assertive, and certainly not selfish! And yet, here was that dream character who was all three of these women morphed onto one.

Upon closer examination, I admitted that there were times when I did things for other people but resented it. Rather than being genuinely generous, I was not always giving out of the goodness of my heart; sometimes I was doing it for approval. Although I did not like it, I could see that this was a self-centered intention rather than a pure act of service. The dreams helped me to see that I had the ability to be assertive, and that there were times when I needed to become more purposeful in my giving, thus healing the resentment. The dreams helped me to see my own attitudes so that I could bring out the generosity in myself. As I made these changes, this dream character ceased appearing in my dreams. Because I changed, my dreams changed.

Why was the dream-person a combination of three people in my waking life rather than just being one person? I think it is because at each of these periods in my life, I needed to understand this quality, to understand the value of being centered in myself, rather than denying myself. I chose to associate with people in my waking life who exhibited a quality I wanted to understand so that I could learn to build it in myself. When I did not produce the understanding in junior high school with my friend Ellen, I chose to be friends with Jamie in college who was similar so that I could learn it through association with her. When I still had not completed the understanding, I was drawn to Allison at the summer program who had a similar quality.

This is another way that our dream characters can educate us: bringing to our attention the qualities that we want or need to learn, which can then help us to see why we have chosen certain relationships in our waking lives.

Is it You or is it Me?

Oftentimes, dreamers want to believe that a dream character is the actual person in waking life rather than a symbolic representation of an aspect of the self. This is especially true when the dreamer has romantic fantasies about a particular person, and in the dream the object of the dreamer's affection is showing interest in the dreamer!

Like the young dreamer mentioned in the beginning of this chapter, people may dream of someone on whom they have a "crush," hoping the dream means that the other person likes them. The principle I have learned is that every person in a dream represents an aspect of the dreamer. The object of the dreamer's affection represents a particular quality, so it is that quality to which the dreamer is attracted. This is why many people tend to be attracted to the same type of person repeatedly — they want to understand and build within themselves what they are drawn to in that "type."

This is a helpful perspective, because it can aid us to exercise more reason in our choices rather than feeling helplessly drawn to a particular person without knowing why. When we understand what we see in the other person, we can develop it within ourselves, becoming more fulfilled.

Such knowledge may alleviate fears. Sometimes people dream that a spouse is having an affair. Does this mean the spouse is cheating in waking reality? Probably not. In most cases, the dreamer is experiencing challenges with self-trust. The dreamer doubts his or her ability to fulfill the desires of the self. He has difficulty expecting that the subconscious mind will give him what he wants, or she doubts her ability to be committed to what she says she will do. This lack of commitment to self shows up as a spouse who is uncommitted, because the spouse in the dream symbolizes the dreamer's own subconscious mind or inner self.

Knowing this might save a marriage! I knew a couple once who went to counseling because the wife heard the husband mumbling in his sleep. He was dreaming of another woman and the wife thought that he was having an affair. In truth, the husband was faithful and his dreams were about an aspect of himself that this other woman symbolized. When the wife learned more about the meaning of the dreams she ceased being angry with her husband.

Soul Mates

Do you remember the song called "Mr. Sandman"?

"Mr. Sandman, bring me a dream. Make him the cutest that I've ever seen. Give him two lips like roses and clover. Then tell him that his lonesome nights are over. Sandman, I'm so alone. Don't have nobody to call my own. Please turn on your magic beam. Mr. Sandman, bring me a dream..."[1]

Songs like this, fairy tales, and romantic movies stimulate the desire for a soul mate to come to us in our dreams. I know a couple who have been married for 50 years. The husband says that he knew the minute he met his wife that he was going to marry her, and he even told her that when they first met. As they tell the story, she laughed at him and said, "In your dreams!" He said that he recognized her from his dreams, and that was how he knew she was intended to be his beloved. After 50 years it is clear that they are still in love with each other.

Some people can "see" the future as lines of probability. We have free will, so we can change the future by making different choices, but we can also foresee where things are headed, both in waking clairvoyance and in nighttime dreams. How do we know when, in a dream, we are experiencing a person as an aspect of the self and when it is a precognition?

The developed skill of intuition comes through practice. I have found that precognitive dreams have a feeling in the dream itself of being real. They are usually consistent — things in the dream appear as they are in waking life. When there is inconsistency, often the dream is symbolic. Sometimes we can receive value from interpreting the dream both symbolically and as a message for the future.

Prior to becoming involved romantically with the man I married, we were friends. In fact, both of us were involved in relationships with other people at the time we met and were therefore "unavailable." Yet, we were drawn to each other with a deep soul resonance which I attribute partly to past life recognition. (We learned later, from a past life intuitive report, that we had a significant past life together when we were married in Palestine around 100 A.D.)

At one point in our developing friendship, I dreamed:

I am walking on a path. I see John and am strongly attracted to him. He is watering a flower garden. I am struck by his blue eyes and the warmth that emanates from him.

When I woke up from this dream, I could feel the strong attraction. I wanted to understand it, so I considered what it was about John that resonated in me. I saw him as warm, affectionate, with a light-hearted sense of humor. I recognized that these qualities were ones that I had also sensed in my father, who died when I was a teenager. My father stimulated me to express joy. I was much more affectionate and playful when he was around. When he died, those qualities seemed to become dormant within me.

The dream showed me why I was attracted to John. I was drawn to those qualities in him. It revealed that they were alive in me and just needed to be watered, to flower. An interesting element of the dream was the blue eyes. In waking physical reality, John had brown eyes. That feature helped me to recognize that the *dream-John* was an aspect of myself. I wasn't dreaming about him, I was dreaming about my need to express the warmth and affection in myself.

I applied the dream by practicing to become more light-hearted, warmer, and more affectionate. I learned how to tell jokes. I tried not to take myself so seriously, learning to be less critical of myself. As a result, my relationships changed. Eventually John and I ended the partnerships with our respective girlfriend and boyfriend. Our friendship with each other developed into romance and marriage.

The *dream-John* aided me to understand a quality in myself that I needed to develop and in so doing, I became more whole.

One of the reasons why dreams of romance are so profound is that there is an urge within each of us to become whole. As it is written in some scriptures and mythology, in writings of Plato, the soul in the beginning was whole. It split, and now as we exist in physical form, we are always searching for our "other half," the inner self from which we are disconnected.

In Plato's "Symposium," he describes it:

"...human nature was originally one and we were a whole, and the desire and pursuit of the whole is called love."[2]

We search to become whole in relationships and we can use relationships to bring out of ourselves the qualities that lie dormant within us. In our dreams, the people to whom we are romantically attracted are those aspects of ourselves we want and need to love.

Dream Classes

Some dreams may be inner level connections with other entities. People can meet in the dream state or subconscious mind, either through intentional choice or through chance. People can incubate dreams to attend classes on the inner levels or to meet for particular purposes. Even in these dreams, the dreamer can interpret what the other people represent.

How does one know when the dream is purely symbolic and when there is an inner level connection? Sometimes it has to do with the intention of the dreamer. If, for example, I intend to meet with my class for an inner level teaching, and then have a dream in which the students are gathered together, it probably indicates that those souls or entities are meeting. If the students are also intentionally setting up the experience of attending class, it is a mutual dream projection.

There are times when people dream the same dream but only discover after the fact that they experienced the same thing. This is also known as a dream projection, where the dreamers have projected their consciousness to the same place in subconscious mind.

One of the benefits of keeping a dream journal is to keep a record of such experiences. This aids dreamers to know what has occurred, and to learn through experience how to recognize the inner level meetings. Some dreamers look for a sign. For example, when awake the dreamer focuses on his hand, with the intention of becoming aware when he sees the hand in a dream that he is dreaming. This can also be done with a dream class or dream meeting. Two or more dreamers may agree to meet in a particular place, knowing that when that place appears in the dream that they will be together.

Recording the results and then comparing the records aids dreamers to validate their experiences and to recognize in the future when they are dreaming together.

Visitations

Many people are curious about visitation dreams. A visitation is a dream in which a deceased person comes to visit the dreamer or when the dreamer visits the one who has passed away. One indication of a visitation dream is the method of communication from the person who is no longer incarned. When it is a direct appearance, the deceased person may not speak verbally in the dream. The communication may be in gestures (he or she won't say anything but will be reported by the dreamer as "just being there,") or the communication will be telepathic, a mind-to-mind thought transference.

How is this possible? Death is not an end to existence; it is a change in consciousness and form. As I understand the process of death, it is a withdrawal of consciousness from the physical body and brain. The soul or spirit of the entity continues to live in the inner levels of existence, the subconscious mind. This is the same place we go when we sleep at night. In fact, the process of going to sleep is very similar; it is a withdrawal of consciousness and attention from the physical body and brain to direct the awareness inward into the subconscious mind.

The realm of dreams is the same realm in which we exist after death, or in-between lives for those who believe in multiple lives.

Sometimes, when a loved one has died, the dreamer yearns for a visitation dream that does not happen. The dreamer needs to be patient, to give the one who has "withdrawn" the time to get used to existence on the "other side." Just as a new-born baby needs to adjust to life in a physical form, learning to move its limbs, become familiar with making sounds and interacting with other people, so when a person dies he or she needs a period of adjustment to get used to being in the new existence without a physical body. The soul needs time to assimilate the life just lived. The entity may not yet be ready to communicate with those who are still alive. For this reason, we may not have visitation dreams from those who have died. It is important to be patient and respect the process of transition.

One dreamer had the following dream three months after her daughter's father died: "My daughter's 11th birthday was yesterday. Her father died three months ago. Although we never married, I always loved him."

Last night I think he visited me; he was talking to me, but not in words. Saying that I could visit him this way, and I asked if I have to die to see him again. He "said" no, that I just have to do this...meaning visiting in dreams with him. He was happy and playful. A couple weeks ago I dreamed I was in a building, very white and clean, and he was there sleeping. "They" (people I never saw but understood were communicating with me) said I need to leave him alone, that he was just sleeping. I felt like I needed to get out and leave him alone. [3]

45

This dream was a clear message to the dreamer that she was in contact with the man she loved and that she could have future contact with him in her dreams. Like many visitation dreams, she experienced him as being happy, released from the body and existing in a state of natural freedom. The previous dream shows that the man is still assimilating his new life; this is why in the dream he is sleeping and she needs to leave him alone, so that he can go through his own process.

Most people experience a state of peace in visitation dreams, the sense that the departed loved one is doing well and wishes the dreamer well. In many cases, the entity who has died comes to reassure the dreamer that he or she is okay.

In the chapter of this book entitled "Inner Level Communication," I describe a couple of profound visitation dreams that brought me great peace. I hope that all people who are grieving have at least one such dream to give them the experience of love beyond death!

People Are More Important Than Things

I have a friend who taught her son when he was little, "People are more important than things." He used to repeat this, and it was a good reminder to me to give my undivided attention to the people in my life. Too many people try to "multi-task," answering emails or doing other things while talking on the phone, sending text messages when in the presence of another person. No wonder so many people are unfulfilled in their relationships!

We can learn about ourselves through giving and receiving, through the exchange of energy that occurs in mutual creation. Whether we are building a family, developing a business with a partner, or creating an art project with our friends, our associations give us opportunities to learn, grow, change, and understand more completely who we are.

Every relationship can enrich us because we learn more about how to love and be loved. What might happen if each night before sleep we evaluate how we have grown in our understanding of love? Our dreams can give us feedback on this process, so that we can start each day with a renewed determination to be our best, to give and receive, and to improve the lives of everyone we touch.

Our dream characters show us how.

Beyond Edgar Cayce:
Dream "prescriptions"
in Intuitive Health and Past Life Readings

In the early 1900's, well-known psychic Edgar Cayce stumbled upon a method for obtaining knowledge directly from an etheric source known as the Akashic Records. Cayce, sometimes known as the "sleeping prophet," reported information from a trance-like state to improve the health and well-being of people wanting to become more whole.

As described on the Edgar Cayce Foundation website, the readings came from "an etheric source of information, called the 'Akashic Records,' which is apparently some kind of universal database for every thought, word, or deed that has ever transpired in the earth..."

The website also describes Cayce's ability to put aside the conscious mind so that the information could be given:

"In this state the conscious mind becomes subjugated to the subconscious, superconscious or soul mind; and may and does communicate with like minds, and the subconscious or soul force becomes universal..."[1]

In the present day, intuitive researchers at the School of Metaphysics have developed a method of Intuitive Reports similar to the readings done by Edgar Cayce. Past Life reports from the Akashic Records and Intuitive Health Analyses are done by a reader-conductor team. The reader, known as the "intuitive reporter," uses methods of spiritual discipline to slow down the breath and heartbeat and enter a kind of meditative state. The conductor directs her attention to the correct place in mind. The intuitive reporter is "asleep" and reports the knowledge directly from the etheric source, much like Edgar Cayce did. In this way, the opinions or value judgments of the person "reporting" the information do not interfere with the knowledge being retrieved. The School of Metaphysics' intuitive reporters and conductors volunteer their time and energy to provide this service, thus insuring that the knowledge is pure and free from any taint of ego or self-aggrandizement.

The SOM's intuitive reports are designed to respect each person's right to think, so they do not make decisions for people. They offer an objective soul-centered perspective that enables people to view themselves more holistically. They can guide and instruct; however, it is up to each person to decide for him or herself what s/he considers to be true.

Since the late 1960's, these intuitive reports have served tens of thousands of people around the world. A significant number of these readings recommend that people remember and record dreams, using the knowledge obtained in the dream-state for soul development, health, healing, and understanding. In some cases, individuals are counseled to interpret the dreams, and in others, the simple act of increasing awareness of the dream-state produces greater health.

Some people wonder if dreams have meaning and how important it is to remember them. We can find objective answers to these questions in this etheric source of knowledge. The Akashic Records can be described as a universal library in vibratory form. The Health Aura emanates from the essence of the entity being "read" and gives an inner level picture of that person's needs. Although the knowledge in each intuitive report is designed for the individual who requests it, the wisdom has universal applications. Most of the "dream prescriptions" give holistic suggestions that can be applied for the goodness of all concerned.

There is vast knowledge available to us from this etheric source and it seems significant that the subconscious mind itself recommends dreams as a source of healing and soul development. Some intuitive reports describe how dreams can be used for deeper understanding of the self and the soul, to strengthen creativity, to improve communication and friendship, for greater physical health, for emotional healing, and for understanding one's purpose in life. Individuals who gain access to this inner source of knowledge may increase their ability to be whole and to be a healing presence for others.

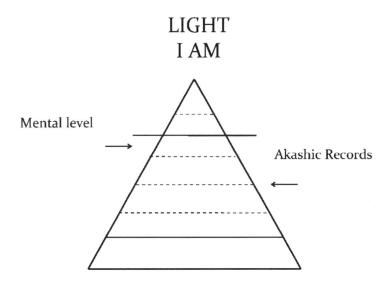

You have seen the diagram of the mind in a previous chapter. You will note that in the subconscious mind there are four levels. The third, or innermost level of the subconscious mind, is where the health aura is "read." An Intuitive Health Analysis is designed to relate any disorders, mental, emotional, or physical, and also relate those things necessary for the correction of disorders.

The Akashic Records exist between the 4th and 5th levels of consciousness. When a person requests a significant Past Life Profile or two people request a Past Life Crossing, the knowledge comes from this place. The School of Metaphysics respects the rights of people to choose for themselves whether or not they want this knowledge; thus, we only give intuitive reports for people who request them and and give their permission with a signature.

Significant Past Life Profile

You might look at life as a kind of schoolroom. A soul "incarns" or comes into a physical body for the purpose of learning to grow compatible with our Maker. From this perspective, all of our life experiences can be used to develop greater understanding of who we are and who we can become. The idea of reincarnation (which means, literally, "back in the flesh again") is that a soul comes into the flesh, or physical body, in each lifetime for the purpose of continuing its growth.

The School of Metaphysics Past Life Profiles identify one particular lifetime that is significant to an individual at a given time because of its resonance with the soul lesson he or she needs to learn. It is as if we go through grades in the schoolroom of life, and when we have an incomplete lesson, we seek other opportunities to learn it, whether in one lifetime or the next. Karma is a way to describe these lessons or understandings we need to fulfill.[2]

Here is an excerpt from a Past Life Profile for a man who requested it because he wanted to know his purpose life. He was having a kind of "mid-life crisis." In the significant past lifetime, he tried to please his (past life) father by choosing an occupation he thought his father wanted him to pursue. It was not what he wanted for himself. No matter what he did, he could not win his father's approval. In the present lifetime, the intuitive reported suggested:

> We see within the present time period that this one has at times felt that what this one wanted was at odds with the spirit... there is an internal sense of this, where this one is often unsure of how to cooperate with the inner self and the ability to align the outer consciousness with the inner soul purpose or drive.
>
> **We see that there could be benefit derived from this one studying the dreams, beginning to remember**

the dreams, beginning to be attentive to the dreams, beginning to understand their qualities, and respond to them. This would establish an inner rapport that often eludes this one, and it would enable this one to have the internal guidance as well in terms of what the dream states can offer the self. This would then aid this one in becoming more fulfilled in the choices that this one makes. (12-9-2009-BGC-3)

As in the past lifetime, this man has some challenges knowing who he is and what fulfills him. The recommendation about being attentive to dreams surprised him, as he had never given them much thought. He was intrigued by the idea that listening to dreams could help him hear the call of his soul.

The next Past Life Profile is included here in its entirety, because it is highly instructive. In the significant past life, the young woman's grandmother died. When her grandmother appeared in her dreams, it helped ease her distress. The challenge she faced was knowing the difference between her imagination and perception. She did not know when she was experiencing an actual visitation (awake or asleep) and when she was imagining it because she missed her grandmother.

In the present life, she has a similar challenge. She gets lost in her imagination and confuses it with perception. The part of the reading that asks, "What is the significance of that lifetime to the present lifetime for this entity?" suggests that she practice lucid dreaming as a way to strengthen her conscious mind skills.

There is such rich wisdom in this intuitive report I want to share it in its complete form.

You will search for the identity of the entity referred to as KMV and relate a significant incarnation for this entity.

This one is in female form. This one is in the area referred to as Japan. This one lives on the coast and the family is involved in fishing. This one does not have many responsibilities early in the life. The living is easy and open. There is much frolicking upon this one's part and very little disturbs this one. There is joy and there is interaction with others, particularly around this one's age. Most of the life is seen as play or game; nothing is taken too seriously.

Then the grandmother dies, this being the person that this one was closest to. This one does not understand this. This one does not understand parting. This one believes that others are taking her grandmother away from her and this one enters into a denial of culminations, completions, endings. After that, this one will not admit, or endure or suffer any mention of the grandmother, nor will this one acknowledge when there is a parting. This one instead enters into her own imagination that things continue and that they continue in a fashion that is to her liking. **This one then becomes confused because there are visitations from the grandmother that this one experiences in the dream state, particularly, and some are in visions as well. However, this one does not know how to distinguish between her imagination and perception, and therefore this one finds that she is more and more isolated. She finds that she cannot talk about her experiences with other people because they do not understand them.** *They reprimand her or they make fun of her, and she becomes trapped in her own imaginings, for we see that others believe that she is merely making stories up and the ones who will listen don't believe her.*

In time, and as this one ages, this one decides that she will not speak of such things and it does not keep this one from experiencing them; however, this one learns not to share them. And in time, others forget or set aside their judgments of her and we see that this one is able to move in the society easily.

We see that this one is actually quite bright, and this one does end up inventing certain ways to fashion netting that helps the family business. She is viewed as having two entirely separate personalities or parts of herself. One is the more creative, inventive, practically-minded and helpful daughter or sister, and the other is the recluse, the loner, the unstable individual. Because of the latter, this one does not marry. There are those within the village and they know her past and there is some concern that she might have children and pass this on to others. This is a local belief.

It becomes more difficult as other people leave or die for this one to reconcile the thoughts that have been described earlier and eventually this one ends up moving into a type of dream world, whereby this one finds it difficult to distinguish inner and outer realities. It is because of this that ultimately leads to this one's death, for this one becomes distracted, and does not place enough attention upon the physicality of the self and the safety of the self and from this one's own neglect in that regard, this one ends up causing her own demise. This is at the age of 36. She is referred to as Suka Tanamito. The time period would be 1200. This is all.

Very well, what would be the significance of that lifetime to the present lifetime for this entity?

Once again, we see for this one to have an active imagination, and we see for this one to oftentimes confuse it with perceptions that this one is capable of having. **There would be benefit from this learning how to direct the mind in the dream state. Being practiced or versed in lucid dreaming would aid this one greatly, for it would require this one to develop and utilize the conscious mind and will in order for there to be interaction with the subconscious mind.** *There is a need for this one to keep the two separate and to recognize the duties and offices of both and to utilize the consciousness in that regard. We see that this one has potential for interpretation of energies, perception, that could be most helpful, not only to the self but to others as well. Therefore, the honing of this ability into a skill would be most helpful in regards to her own soul growth and progression and that of others.*

The need for this one to understand the difference between perception and imagination is long-standing within this one, and we see that this one has built some understandings between the past lifetime related and the present that can be called upon in this work. Would suggest that this one not become discouraged merely because there is something that this one does not understand. **Understanding is the reason for this one being in the earth plane.** *Therefore, this one's willingness to choose experiences for the purpose of understanding would accelerate the transition process that is being spoken of here.*

There is also once again the tendency for this one to have a kind of emotional allergy to endings. There is once again the tendency toward denial. Would suggest that this one become more cognizant of this and begin to recognize that everything in its cycle has a beginning and an end, that it is only the understandings in the experience that will endure. Once this is understood by the self, this one will have much less reaction to culminations, completeness, and what this one would see as death. This is all. (6-5-2010-BGC-5)

The wisdom in this intuitive report can be of great benefit to dreamers everywhere. It shows how helpful it is when people can share their psi experiences without feeling like they are crazy or alone. It is also important to distinguish between that which is a direct perception or visitation and when it is "wishful thinking." As this Past Life Profile suggests, practicing lucid dreaming can hone the development of conscious will which enables people to know how to interpret their experiences.

One of the clearest statements of the purpose of life is in this intuitive report: "Understanding is the reason for this one being in the earth plane. Therefore, this one's willingness to choose experiences for the purpose of understanding would accelerate the transition."

Intuitive Health Analysis

An Intuitive Health Analysis relates all "disorders as seen, whether mental, emotional, or physical" and also relates "those things necessary for the correction of any disorder." These are a valuable resource for identifying attitudes that are out of balance. When the mind is out of alignment, the energetic system and the physical body follow suit.[3]

Intuitive research has shown that physical disorders start in the mental system. The book **Permanent Healing** by Dr. Daniel Condron gives specific cause-and-effect relationships between mental attitudes and the disorders they foster.[4]   Permanent healing comes from an "attitude adjustment," correcting unhealthy ways of thinking. The Intuitive Health Analysis gives suggestions for causing productive change, mentally and emotionally. It also recommends diet, exercise, or other holistic methods for symptomatic relief.

This excerpt from an Intuitive Health Analysis shows how nutritional supplements can support the body, and how remembering dreams can have a direct effect on the endocrine system to produce healing.

We see within the physical body there is sluggishness in the area of the thyroid, hypothalamus and pituitary. Would suggest the intake of kelp, iodine, shellfish, vitamin A, vitamin D, and vitamin C. Ginkgo will be of some benefit. Would suggest the use of visualization on a daily basis. This will aid in correcting the condition in the pituitary and hypothalamus. **It would benefit this one as well to remember and record the dreams in order to stimulate this area.**
(3-12-1996-LJC-3)

The person who received this health analysis was amazed to learn that keeping a dream journal could have such a profound effect on the body as well as the mind.

Creative Mind

Most people feel energized and fulfilled when they are invested in creative thinking. The Creative Mind intuitive report describes how someone engages his conscious and subconscious minds together to create and fulfill desires.[5] This excerpt is from a Creative Mind report given for a young man who is quite imaginative and intelligent, but often feels stymied because he has difficulty manifesting his brilliant ideas in his life.

The intuitive report described why his mind is barren. It suggested he learn to think in pictures to draw more completely upon subconscious mind. It said that dreams could offer him a way to do that:

> *We see that this one resides in the brain and therefore there is the attempt to associate, to create, to connect, to cause mental motion through brain patterns. This is highly frustrating for this one ... this one remains in the thinking processes and does move in rapid fashion ideas that have no substance, that have no bearing or relevance to the inner mind. Therefore, these ideas tend to be barren ...*

> *Would suggest that this one begin to define the self by something other than his ideas, and to base his assessment of self and others upon more permanent virtues or characteristics. This would be an excellent exercise to aid this one in becoming free of the old patterns of thinking that this one so easily falls prey to.*

> ***We see that it would also be important for this one to be attentive to the dreams, for this one needs to learn how to think in pictures.*** *This one has the ability to visualize in the physical conscious mind. However, this one does not understand the relationship between the outer and inner mind, as the essence of visualization, and therefore the intelligence of creativity. As this one is able to slow the mind, so that there can be so that there can be images which the words and actions describe, there will then be the ability to* ***think with the mind rather than the brain.***

The Creative Mind report describes how someone draws upon intuition, bringing forth from the subconscious mind the energy that manifests into physical form. In this part of the intuitive report, this young man was again counseled to use the dreams for deeper understanding of the process of creating with the inner mind:

Very well. You will also relate that which will foster a movement

within the energy exchange between the ethereal and the material for the cultivation of genius.

This would be in the stilling of the conscious mind, the development of the willpower to be able to keep the attention in the present and upon what is at hand. The development of concentration is essential for this one. The ability to hold the mind steady is important, and we see that this needs to be done with thought as well as with things. We see that there is a need to develop the ability to perceive in pictures, to then describe them with words as has already been given.

The development and use of dream states would aid this as well.

There is a need for this one to begin to practice the receiving of other people's images. This is very challenging for this one, for we see that this one allows the mind to be busy and in doing so does not allow the impression on his mind substance of images from other people. Therefore, this one remains within his own thinking. Part of this is a defensive, protective device. Part of it is a means by which this one can maintain the distance between the self and others that this one finds more comfortable. This one is still attached to separation, and as long as this idea is ruling the self, there will continue to be separation between the inner and outer self as well. Therefore, in order to utilize more of the mind than is presently being done, this will need to be changed. This is all. (10-18-2002-BGC-8)

Divine Friendship

Most people who invest their time and energy in dreamwork find that they get to know themselves as soul or spirit. The dreaming experience awakens us to metaphysical existence – the reality beyond the physical body. This can aid us to become better friends, to develop relationships that extend beyond familiar patterns of behavior.

A Friendship Portrait is a special intuitive report given at Spiritual Focus Sessions at the College of Metaphysics, designed to aid people understand how they approach relationships. Sometimes people assume that everyone looks at friendship the same way, when, in fact, people operate under different paradigms regarding associations. When we become aware of the expectations that govern our relationships, we can be better friends, colleagues, and partners.

One woman learned that dreams could help her relate to people on a deeper level, thereby having more fulfilling friendships.

This one approaches associations with others as a means of archetypal images. There are ways in which this one has created structures in the thinking that define relationships between people. This one then functions from these structures, the beliefs, and the ideas this one has attached to them. There is a very strong sense of self-identity that is involved in this, and this one does see the self in certain ways and does know the self in certain ways. It is from this place that this one chooses to interact with others depending upon the archetypal forms that they supply her.

We see that this is an opportunity for this one to expand the thinking and to recognize existence beyond the physical level of consciousness. We see that there is the tendency for this one to become caught up in the physicality of the self when this one tries to consciously enter into associations with others.

When this one is more mindful and is functioning more from the inner mind then this one begins to perceive and to honor the relationships with others in a more universal sense.

It will be most helpful for this one to understand the night-time dreams, the dreams that are initiated from the inner self, to begin to understand the language of consciousness and mind, and to be able to interpret what this one perceives in that light.
(7-9-2009-BGC-1)

Curiosity and Wonder

People who explore dreams seem to be fascinated with mystery. Wondering what happens when we sleep is a first step in developing the curiosity to remember and understand dreams. As a teacher of metaphysics, I teach students to keep a dream journal to record their soul progression. At the School of Metaphysics, dream work is fundamental to becoming aware of one's existence as a spiritual being.

Sometimes students have challenges remembering their dreams. They may have, at one time, been taught that dreams are "just imagination," and therefore not worth considering. Or they may have developed a long-standing habit of ignoring dreams because they jump out of bed ready to plunge into the day's activities. Occasionally a student realizes that she is not remembering because she is afraid.

A woman who began her metaphysical studies in her late 50's realized that she had some fear that was keeping her from remembering her dreams, so she asked about it in a Creative Mind intuitive report:

What am I fearing about remembering dreams?

> *That this one would become aware of the need for change before this one is willing to make the change. ... This one is reluctant to change in the conscious mind and is battling the Self in that regard, and this has been a process of shutting out the inner Self. It is the shutting out of the inner Self that has produced the battle. Therefore, when this one begins to create the conditions necessary in the outer consciousness for there to be attunement to the inner, the battle will cease and there will be an entirely new level of experience that this one has not had since childhood. (5-10-2003-BGC-1)*

This suggestion changed the woman's life. She started to cry when she heard that "there will be an entirely new level of experience that this one has not had since childhood." It was as if she were a flower that had closed to protect itself from the elements. This knowledge gave her permission to change, to

61

open like a bud unfolding its petals to the light. Since receiving this, her dream life has been more active, and she is anticipating even greater communion with her inner Self as she becomes more familiar with her dreams.

Dreams and intuitive reports are doorways for exploring the inner levels of consciousness. Both reveal a transcendent vision of humanity's potential. Although the universal knowledge in the Akashic Records is available to anyone, conscious access requires a developed practice of spiritual discipline. People who have not exercised their minds in this way can receive intuitive reports from a trained conductor-intuitive reporter team, either at a distance, or in person at Spiritual Focus Sessions on the campus of the College of Metaphysics in Missouri, USA. To learn more about the Society for Intuitive Research, a division of the School of Metaphysics, you can visit the school's website.[6] Its purpose is to accelerate the evolution of humanity through drawing upon the timeless wisdom of the subconscious mind.

Healing
Dreams

The Voice-Over Dream

"If you build it, they will come." — The Voice (from *Field of Dreams*)

Some years ago I was writing a book on visualization, a revision of a book that I had written in 1994 called **Shaping Your Life: The Power of Creative Imagery**. The original book had gone out of print, and several people told me that its title was not descriptive enough. Some people thought it was a fitness book, or a book on artistic creativity.

After spending several years on the new book, revising it, adding intuitive research, updating some of the stories, I was pleased with the content but didn't have a title that satisfied me. Conceiving the perfect title is perhaps the most difficult part for me in writing a book. I brainstormed. I researched other books on visualization. I wrote pages of possible book titles in notebooks. I scribbled potential title ideas on the backs of envelopes and notepads and scraps of paper.

One evening I gave a lecture on visualization based on this book that was not yet published. I asked the audience if they had ideas for book titles. They shouted out suggestions, but none was suitable. So that night, I decided to incubate a dream. If my conscious mind wasn't coming up with the perfect title, maybe I could dream it up!

I wrote down in my dream journal, "Please give me a dream with the title for my book on visualization." The next morning, as I was waking up, in that hypnopompic state preceding full awakening, in my mind I heard these words: *"The Law of Attraction and Other Secrets of Visualization."* I wrote it down in my dream notebook. When I became fully awake and read what I recorded, I thought, "What a boring title for a book!" However, I knew that I had asked my dreams for it and so I decided I had better trust it. I used it for the book's title, exactly as I dreamed it. It turned out to be very effective. In fact, the book sold out in the first year of publication and went into a second printing the first year.

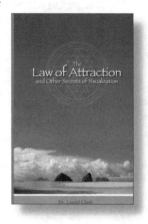

That experience was very compelling to me. When I asked a direct question, I received a direct answer and I realized the importance of trusting what I received.

Intrigued, I started exploring similar occurrences with this voice that came forward in dreams. The first time I

remembered this happening, I was in my early twenties. For some unknown reason I was completely fatigued and had great difficulty waking up in the morning. I wasn't sick; I would just wake up in the morning, turn off my alarm and fall back to sleep. It was troubling to me because I didn't know why I was so tired and sluggish. I felt bad about myself but kept experiencing it.

One morning when it happened once again, I asked myself wearily, "Why am I so tired?" and dozed off. All of a sudden, I was jolted awake by a voice that sounded like it was yelling in my ear. It told me in no uncertain terms, *"You need to set goals!"* It was stern and authoritative. I was startled and looked around, because it was so loud I thought there was someone in my room shouting at me. I paid attention. Immediately I got up and made a list of goals. I made that a daily practice, setting goals, taking action on them, and reviewing them before going to bed at night for the next day. I was completely energized after that.

These two experiences stimulated my curiosity. Are these actually dreams? What is that voice? Where does it come from? Whose voice is it? Why do some dreams come in that form when others are so visual?

I wondered if this is a universal phenomenon. Are people known as auditory learners more prone to experience this type of dream? Do they occur only at certain times? I put out a call to people I know who work with dreams. I asked people on the internet. One respondent was Dr. Lou Hagood, a psychoanalyst in New York City. Dream incubation is his primary form of spiritual practice. He said that he has dreams like this when he incubates a dream with a precise question. Reflecting on my own experiences, I found that that was also true for me. When I incubated a dream with a very specific question, then I received a voice dream with a very specific answer. It is as if the subconscious mind wants to get the message across, clearly, with no confusion and no ambiguity. As it says in the **Bible**, "Ask, and ye shall receive."

I have found that the answers seem to come upon awakening. Not in the beginning, or the middle of a dream, but upon awakening, in that half-asleep, half-awake state. I learned that there is name for it: the hypnopompic state. The hypnogogic state is when you are just going to sleep. Hypnopompic is when you are just waking up. The people I've asked, both at the International Association for the Study of Dreams conference in the Netherlands and in other places, universally report that these voice dreams happen upon awakening. I have found for myself that these voice messages have clear and unmistakable answers. They are not vague or nebulous or veiled. They are straightforward and direct.

When I gave this presentation at the IASD Conference of 2011, a remarkable number of people came to me with their own experiences that supported the personal research I had done.

One directed me to the writings and work of C.G. Jung, who considered "The Voice" of dreams to contain insight superior to the intellect. An October 1937 article published in *The New York Times* quotes Dr. Jung from a lecture given at Yale on the subject:

"As a result of analyzing dreams of this type, Dr. Jung said that he must admit that the unconscious mind was capable of assuming an intelligence and purposiveness which were superior to actual conscious insight.

'The "Voice" is always a matter of an authoritative declaration or command, either of astonishing common sense and truth, or of profound philosophic allusion,' he said. 'It is nearly always a definite statement, usually toward the end of a dream and it is, as a rule, so clear and convincing that the dreamer finds no argument against it. It has, indeed, so much the character of indisputable truth that it often appears as the final and absolutely valid summing up of a long unconscious deliberation and weighing of arguments. Frequently the Voice issues from an authoritative figure, as from a military commander, or the captain of a ship, or an old physician. Sometimes there is simply a Voice coming apparently from nowhere.'"[1]

I would describe such figures as superconscious aspects of the self. These are people with authority, symbolizing in a dream the higher authority or universal truth coming from superconscious mind.

The mind is not the same as the physical brain. The mind is a vehicle that serves as a way for consciousness to express itself. At your center is Light, or awareness. I understand the "Self" to be that individual spark of awareness known as I AM. In the *Bible*, it says, "Be still and know that I AM God." In stillness we discover the Real Self at the core of our being.

The inner most or highest part of the mind is our inherent divinity, the superconscious mind. Some people might call this the spirit. I believe that in each of us there is a Divine Plan for our existence that resides in superconscious mind. The conscious and subconscious minds serve the High Self or superconscious mind. As I see it, when our conscious choices align with the Divine Plan in superconscious mind, we live a fulfilling life. We experience miracles, synchronicity, benevolent happenings.

The inner self is the subconscious mind where dreaming occurs. The outer self is the conscious mind. In my understanding of visualization, the conscious mind forms the direct question or idea. That question, such as the one I asked, "What should I call this book?" is like a seed that the conscious mind plants in subconscious mind by turning the question over to the dream for an answer.

When that seed idea is planted in the subconscious mind it grows, and in its development it brings to us the answers we seek, like a seed that produces flowers or vegetables in a garden. I understand visualization to work in a similar fashion: the conscious and subconscious minds work together as partners. The subconscious mind's duty is to fulfill the conscious mind's desires. I love this concept because it means that we have within us an inner self that brings to us what we need.

This is how "coincidence" happens. One thing I appreciate about the IASD conferences is that many people recognize the value of synchronicity — being in the right place at the right time, "just happening" to be with someone who has the resources for something you're seeking, or having a book fall off a shelf that has the answer you've been looking for. I have heard many stories over the past few days of people who have experienced such happenings. I believe that although this occurs frequently, many people ignore it, or doubt the cause-and-effect relationship of their thoughts to the manifestation of them. I think people here pay attention to synchronicity because dreamers are attuned to their subconscious minds. When people are attentive to their dreams, they are more open to these subconscious connections.

In incubating a dream, the question for the dream incubation is like a seed that the conscious mind plants in a garden. If you plant a tomato seed, you get tomatoes. When you plant lettuce seeds, they grow lettuce. That is why the question that you ask is important, because the kind of question influences the answer you receive. If you ask a clear and direct question, you will often receive a clear and unmistakable answer.

As I was exploring this concept, I had a healing dream. I do not consider myself to be a "healer," so this was an unusual kind of message for me. It started with a back injury. I drive a lot in the work that I do. One winter, I had to drive through an ice storm from St. Louis, Missouri to Lexington, Kentucky. I had an appointment that I had already delayed and had to make it to my destination. A trip that usually took four or five hours took about eight hours during the ice storm because the cars were creeping along.

I was really anxious. There were trucks off the side of the road, having spun out of control on the ice. It was kind of crazy, and in retrospect, I should have cancelled the appointment. Instead, I was driving through this ice storm, very tense and scared. The road conditions were horrible. I wasn't about to use cruise control, so I was driving with my foot on the accelerator, with tension in my muscles, for hours.

When I got out of the car my back was completely wrenched and I could hardly even move. As the day wore on I couldn't move at all, so I became alarmed and decided to use my dreams for healing. When I went to bed, before going to sleep I wrote down in my dream journal, "I want to wake up pain free." I added, "Please give me a dream that tells me what I need to do to heal my back."

I went to sleep and when I awoke, miraculously, I was pain free. There was no pain at all in my lower back and I heard this voice in my mind say very clearly and directly, *"Walk backwards."* That  seemed odd to me, but I got up and walked backwards around the house a few times. It felt kind of good.

Later that day I needed to drive again, so I got into the car. I noticed an audio-cassette tape that a friend had given to me a couple of months earlier that I had put in my glove box. I had never listened to it. For some reason unknown to my conscious mind, I decided that day to pop it into the tape player. I listened to the tape, a lecture given by a man who works with healing oils. He was telling a story about his travels to countries where he gets the herbs and flowers to make his oils. He spoke about a place where the people walk backwards because it adjusts their lower spine. That was amazing! It told me that not only was my dream giving me an answer to my query, my subconscious mind was also communicating in my waking state. This is an example of the synchronicity that I mentioned earlier. Consciously I did not know why I decided to listen to the tape that day, but it gave me an affirmation that the dream message was true. So now when I start to feel an ache in my lower back, I walk backwards to help adjust the spine.

(An added note: hearing that tape stimulated me to research Gary Young's website from which I learned that "walking backwards ... changes the rotation in the pelvis, elongating the spine, and decompressing the discs in your back. Thus, you can clear the nerve channels for energy to flow smoothly throughout your brain and body."[2])

As I was preparing for this conference, I wanted to form a conclusion about "The Voice" in dreams. So I decided to incubate a dream to ask these questions, to practice what I am presenting here. I wanted to know, "What is the voice? Where is it coming from?" and, "Whose voice is it?"

I thought about the questions. I wrote them in my dream journal and I woke up with the voice in my mind saying *Hotel Concierge.* When I heard that answer I thought, "Well, this isn't quite the direct answer I was expecting to get." However, I decided to interpret it the way I have learned to interpret dreams.

I understand a hotel in my dream to symbolize Universal Mind. A hotel is a place where there are many different people from different cultures and different countries. They speak different languages. When you look around at all the people staying at this conference center, it is definitely a diverse group, and yet there is something we all have in common. We are all human beings. We all dream.

The concierge is the intelligent one who seems to know everything about the place you are staying. The concierge can tell you where to eat, the best sites to visit, how to find the transportation you need, and so on. So, I understood this message to mean that "The Voice" is the Infinite Intelligence in Universal Mind that has the answers to all our questions.

I do not know if this is a universal answer. I do believe that it is an answer for myself regarding the voice that I hear in my dreams. A woman in the morning dream group that I have been attending during this conference just yesterday told us a dream with a voice message. She gave me permission to share it with you. She and her husband have been on a kind of spiritual journey, facing a life-changing decision about whether they should pick up their lives and move to another part of the country. They were pondering this when she had a Voice dream. Upon awakening she heard a very clear voice that said, "Be still and know that I am God." That, to her, was a direct statement concerning the decision they were making. From her perspective, it was clearly God speaking to her through the dream.

My personal experience and stories like this lead me to the conclusion that when we have a sincere question that we directly ask ourselves, we can receive straightforward answers in our dreams. Whether it comes from Universal Mind, or God, or from a spirit guide (some people view it that way,) it is possible to receive dream-answers that are beyond the scope of our conscious thinking processes.

I am curious to know why certain people have this type of dream-experience and others do not. I am a writer, a speaker, a minister and a counselor, so I pay a lot of attention to words. I always have; as a child I was reading and writing before the age of five. Many of my waking intuitive experiences are auditory, such as hearing thoughts in my mind through telepathy. The voices I hear may be other people's, or sometimes my own. I can easily become distracted by sounds. Music is important to me. Sometimes the words of a song will run through my mind, giving me an answer I'm seeking.

When I first started exploring this topic, my theory was that people who have voice dreams are those who spend a lot of time creating with and focusing upon words. However, by asking people at this conference if they have had voice-message dreams, I have discovered that this is not necessarily true. There are several visual artists with whom I've spoken who have these voice dreams also. It seems like our dreams give us whatever we need so that we get the message.

As Carl Jung wrote (quoted from *Dreams*, translated by R.F.C. Hull) "the phenomenon of the 'voice' in dreams always has for the dreamer the final and indisputable character of [a Greek word loosely translated as authority], i.e., the voice expresses some truth or condition that is beyond all doubt."[3]

When we have a need, the Infinite Intelligence responds. We can facilitate the process by learning how to concentrate. Upon awakening from slumber, lie still and allow the message to come through. Before we start thinking about the upcoming day, it is essential to be mentally still as well. Having a dream journal close at hand to write down what we hear insures that we capture the message as given, before we start analyzing it, second-guessing it or coloring it with doubts. When dreamers pay attention to the loud, clear, commanding Voice that speaks with spiritual authority, we can receive guidance, insight, and direction.

Dream Incubation:
Ancient Science and Modern Art

My eyesight is important. I spend most of my time reading, writing, and driving. So it troubled me when the vision in my right eye became a little blurry and didn't seem to improve. I kept thinking it would go away. When it didn't, I made an appointment with the eye doctor. He said there was nothing wrong with my eye, recommended I use artificial tears if my eyes were dry, and suggested a follow-up appointment. After a few months there was no change, but on the second visit the eye doctor said once again that my eyesight was normal.

On one level, this was a relief; yet, it bothered me that the vision was still not clear. So I decided one night to ask my dreams to give me insight. "What do I need to know to heal my right eye?" I asked my subconscious mind, writing down the question in my dream journal. That night I had the following dream:

> *I ask Karen if a condition I have could be an inner ear infection. She says it could be and suggests ear candling.*

Karen is a friend who is a registered nurse, a certified biofeedback specialist, and quite experienced with the Intuitive Health Analyses conducted by the School of Metaphysics. In my dream she symbolizes an aspect of myself who is knowledgeable about healing. The dream gave me a new perspective. It had never occurred to me that what I thought was an eye problem originated in my ear. I responded by buying ear candles, changing my diet and applying acupressure to the meridian points to reduce the swelling in my sinuses that was probably affecting my eye. Although not completely healed, the condition began to improve as soon as I used the ear candles to clear the infection from my ears.

Asking my subconscious mind to give me a dream for a particular purpose and heeding the response gave me what I needed: guidance beyond the scope of my brain and conscious mind. This is called dream incubation.

Dream incubation is the process of consciously invoking a specific dream or asking a dream to provide an answer to a specific problem or question. Dream incubation is an ancient practice that became prominent in the classical period when dreams were incubated for healing.[1]

In physical science incubation refers to providing the proper conditions for growth and development; for example, incubating a virus in the body or incubating a chick in a special device that keeps the egg warm. As applied to the creative process, incubation may be considered as a time of subconscious reflection. An idea can incubate in the subconscious mind after putting aside the conscious mind research, letting go of preconceived ideas, and letting the brain and conscious mind rest so that the subconscious mind can crystallize or bring together in new ways the insight needed.

Incubating a dream involves a conscious decision to ask for a specific kind of dream (such as a flying dream, or a lucid dream) or asking for a solution to problem (solving a brain teaser or more serious questions like career choices or scientific formulas).

Scholars note that written records of incubating dreams can be traced back to the 3rd millennium B.C. Dream incubation became well known in the temples of the Greek god Asclepius. In ancient Greece, dreams were considered to be divine transmissions; thus, dreams were incubated to receive healing from the god Asclepius. In some cases, the dreamer received healing in the dream and awakened cured. In other cases, Asclepius diagnosed and prescribed treatments in the dream that were administered to the dreamer upon awakening.

In fact, the word "clinic" comes from the Greek "kline," meaning couch or bed, deriving from the practice of preparing a special bed for healing dreams. The symbol of Asclepius, a single snake coiling up a staff, comes from the symbol of the rising kundalini or healing energy.[2]

Dream incubation is reported as a custom in many societies and cultures, including ancient Egypt, Assyria and Mesopotamia, China, American Indian tribes including the Ojibwa, and the Islamic tradition. In modern times, incubation is used for guidance and problem solving. Modern dream researchers and psychologists report the effectiveness of dream incubation.

My own forays into incubating dreams have progressed over the years. The first attempts at incubating dreams were simply asking my subconscious mind to give me dreams that I could remember. Later, it progressed to asking for dreams to give me insight into qualities I wanted to understand, such as love, or gratitude, or peace. As a teacher, I often incubate dreams before a meeting or class or seminar, asking for dreams to give me guidance to serve the needs of my students.

The more dramatic incubation experiences have come from times of intense desire. When writing a book on visualization, I was unsatisfied with any title ideas, so I asked for a dream to give me a good title. With great urgency I asked to "dream up" a title to name the book and help it to sell. This story is in the chapter on "The Voice-Over Dream" in this book. In the same chapter I tell the story of a dream-incubation answer that aided me to heal severe back pain.

I incubated a dream asking my deceased husband to come to me so that I could say "goodbye" in the dream state. I tell this story in the "Inner Level Communication" chapter of this book. I've incubated dreams for the IASD psi contests, asking to receive telepathic messages or to have mutual dreams with other dreamers. I have also used dream incubation in my studies at the School of Metaphysics to hold dream classes at night with my students and to attend dream classes with my teachers. I have asked to become lucid in dreams, or travel to a particular location to meet a friend in the dream state. These are just a few examples of how dream incubation can be used.

How Does Incubation Work?

Both ancient and modern-day incubators report specific steps that are necessary for the incubation process. Metaphysical research on visualization describes how the conscious mind communicates with the subconscious mind to incubate a dream. The conscious mind produces a "seed idea" or intention, then shines mind light upon it by writing, drawing, and preparing with sacred ritual. Relaxing the mind and body enables the dreamer to release the seed idea from the conscious mind so that it can develop, or incubate, in the subconscious mind.

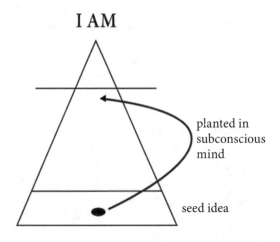

I AM

planted in
subconscious
mind

seed idea

The conscious and subconscious mind work together as partners. When the conscious mind creates a desire, the subconscious mind fulfills it. The subconscious mind is a vast storehouse, which reaches out to all subconscious minds and goes to great lengths to fulfill the conscious mind's desires. We might consider the subconscious mind to be like the internet, reaching out to find as many answers as it can to closely match a search. The dreamer is like the computer operator, for whom formulating the right question to ask the dream is analogous to choosing the best words to put in a search engine.

The law of attraction can be simply described as "like attracts like." In the case of dream incubation, this means that the answer or solution to the incubated question is drawn to us in the form of a dream. Sometimes the answers are clear and direct, in words or direct commands. (Read the chapter on "*The Voice-Over Dream*" for some examples of such dream answers.) Sometimes they may be more symbolic, requiring the dreamer's interpretation to understand the message. I have found that as in any kind of communication, the more clearly I ask the question, the more direct is the answer.

As a student of metaphysics, I practice daily exercises to develop skills in concentration, meditation, and visualization. These practices are effective for dreamers who want to consciously "incept" an idea in their own subconscious mind.

Metaphysics defines "mind" as a whole system that includes the spirit and what some people describe as soul, or inner self. This is understood as separate from the brain and physical neuro-pathways. Incubation begins with the dreamer's conscious imaging. The dreamer formulates a clear idea or question that he or she wants answered from a dream, or an experience that he or wants to have in the dream state. This idea or question must be pictured, or imaged as well as thought in words. The School of Metaphysics describes the "language of the mind" as one of images or pictures.

To plant this idea in the subconscious mind, the dreamer concentrates on the image through practices like drawing and writing. Keeping a dream journal by the bed, and writing the next morning's date, demonstrates an expectation that the dreamer will receive the desired answer or dream experience. The proper mental conditions and the ideal physical conditions, along with a clear expectation of receiving the desired dream answer, are all requirements for successful dream incubation.

These steps combine ancient knowledge with modern practice:

1. **Prepare for sleep mindfully**. It is helpful to remove any distractions from the sleeping place and to withdraw the attention from any kind of stimulation like television or loud music or literature with graphic and strong emotional content. Other suggestions are to refrain from eating after dark and to eliminate stimulants like caffeine or mood-altering drugs or alcohol. Some dreamers find that their dream recall is increased or intensified with nutritional supplements like vitamin B6 and zinc.

2. **Prepare the sleeping place.** The sacred temples of Asclepius were used only for dream incubation. Most modern dreamers do not have the luxury of a place used only for that purpose, but some construct a special tent or wear special pajamas, or place objects by the bedside that are infused with special meaning. Some dreamers choose a particular dreaming stone to hold in their hand as they fall asleep, to concentrate on the desired dream.[3]

It is very helpful to separate the bedroom as a sleeping room and to refrain from using it for watching television or working as a home office. If possible, have the sleeping room infused with sleep-related objects and use a separate room for a living room or work space. Keep the room dark with room-darkening shades or blinds, or keep light out with a sleeping mask to help the body produce melatonin for deeper sleep and dreaming.

3. **Clear the mind**. A concentration exercise is beneficial, like gazing at the tip of a finger or a candle flame. When concentrating on the tip of one's finger, one can form the intention to see the finger in the dream, becoming a kind of sign that the dream-answer is near. Writing down or speaking out loud about any "unfinished business" or worries can also

help clear the mind to prepare for incubating the dream. It is suggested to review the day backwards, drawing out of the memory images like snapshots of the day's events, starting with the most recent and going backwards to the morning. This is like putting files away in their proper places so that the desk is clear for the work at hand.

4. Set a clear intention for the dream incubation. Formulate this as a specific desire. State the intention in a well-defined sentence. Form a **clear mental image** of the desired dream or outcome.

It is especially helpful to ask an **open-ended question** rather than expecting the subconscious mind to make a decision. The the conscious mind holds the decision-making faculty. The subconscious mind can provide understanding and insight. So, for example, if a dreamer wants to incubate a question about moving to a new location, it is better to ask a question like, "What opportunity exists for me in California?" or "What understanding can I gain from moving?" rather than, "Should I move to California?"

5. Do a **stream of consciousness writing** exercise, writing non-stop for 10 – 20 minutes about the desired topic, to clear the brain of any preconceived ideas. Set a timer and then just write. If you find that you are stuck, write something like, "I don't know what to say," and keep on writing. This writing often develops insight, allowing the dreamer to draw forth perceptions that he or she may not have consciously recognized.

6. Draw a picture of the dream incubation topic.

The purpose of writing and drawing about the topic is to engage both left and right brain, or conscious and subconscious minds.

7. **Relax the body**. Deep, rhythmic breathing with muscle relaxation is helpful. Relaxing the body aids the dreamer to remove the attention from the body to go into a deep sleep. It is helpful to lie on one's back, inhale deeply through the nose, hold the breath, and then exhale completely through the mouth. Gently tensing the muscles while holding the breath, and then relaxing the muscles upon exhalation helps to remove bodily tension. Some practitioners progressively tense and relax the muscles of each major muscle group, starting with the feet and going up the body to the top of the head. Finish with a complete exhalation, pushing out all of the air through the mouth. This provides a complete and deep relaxation.

8. **Write down the question or desire for the dream incubation** in a dream notebook. Place the notebook with a pen or pencil by the side of the bed. Date the notebook for the following morning (if the sleep period is at night) or for that day (if the dreamer is taking a daytime nap).

9. Silently or out loud, repeat the dream question over and over, like a **chant** or mantra. This is most effective when done in the drowsy state just prior to falling asleep.

10. **Expect to receive a dream** with the answer to the incubated question, or the kind of dream desired.

11. **Record the dream** in a dream notebook immediately upon awakening. Have the dream notebook within arm's reach so you can write it down without having to move too much.

12. **Heed the message** by acting on the answer in waking life.

The final step of dream incubation is the one most open to debate among modern dream researchers. In ancient times, dream interpretation was a separate function from dream incubation. It was believed that the incubated dream was literal, either with an explicit message or a direct healing. Many modern dream researchers use methods of interpretation to interpret dreams symbolically.

In my education with the School of Metaphysics, I have learned and teach a method of interpreting dreams symbolically with the Universal Language of Mind. When a dreamer incubates a dream, the dream answer is interpreted symbolically as a message providing guidance from the inner self for the dreamer's soul progression. Additionally, in some cases, the incubation response may be a literal answer such as the dreams I reported in the chapter on "*Voice-Over Dreams.*" I received the title to a book I was writing and a clear message for healing some severe back pain, both in audible voice messages rather than in the form of an image.

I know people who have received images of projects they needed to do, a person who dreamed of his future house when he incubated a dream looking for the perfect place to live, and one person who asked for a dream of her future mate and "saw" him before they met in physical waking reality. The metaphysical viewpoint is that dreams may be interpreted multi-dimensionally; in other words, both with a symbolic message and with literal instruction.

Whether they are revealed in direct or symbolic messages, dreams may give us answers to many of life's mysteries. Healing, guidance, prophecy, creative solutions, entrepreneurial discoveries, scientific innovations, and artistic inspiration are just some of the uses of dream incubation.

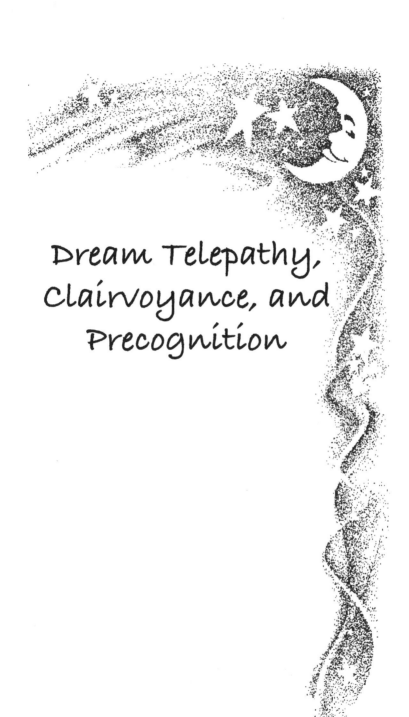

Dream Telepathy, Clairvoyance, and Precognition

Dream Inventions, Inspirations, and Insight

There is an invisible, intangible world that everyone visits every night. We discover new relationships, reconnect with old friends and lovers, meet strangers who seem familiar, and fall in love. In this place, we can experience things we have never seen or touched in our physical life. It can seem supernatural, mystical or otherworldly. It is a universe where the blind can see, the paralyzed can walk, and people can fly without airplanes. This is the world of dreams.

The dream world fascinates people from all walks of life: artists, scientists, writers, counselors, and philosophers. Some of the world's greatest inventions and discoveries came about because of dream helpers. Yet, many people still maintain that they do not dream. Some people think that dreams are meaningless or just the physical result of eating too much pizza before bed.

Understanding dreams is, in itself, a many-layered or multidimensional endeavor. In the media, dreams are often portrayed as crazy fantasies with bizarre scenes that jump chaotically from one to another. Although some people have dreams like that, my experience over three decades, both personally and with hundreds of other dreamers, is that dreams are more often coherent and follow story lines similar to waking life.

The dreaming mind and the physical brain are related. Understanding dreams is a matter of learning about the interconnection of the Self, the mind, and the brain. It seems that the best way to approach dreams is through personal experience. I see this as learning from the inside-out.

How the Media Helps Us

When the subject of dreams arises in the media, it stimulates people to explore their own experiences. Sometimes media attention helps encourage people to talk about happenings that they may have kept to themselves. It opens a door for discussing psi dreams, lucid dreaming, visitations, precognition, or mutual dreaming.

For example, in 2012, an American television series called *Awake* features a police detective who lives and dreams in two worlds after experiencing a car crash. In one world, his wife survives the crash and his teenage son dies; in the other, the son is the survivor and his wife the deceased. Both worlds come together in his waking life when information and images from one dream world appear in the other, helping him to solve crimes.

In both realities, the detective sees a psychiatrist who assures him that he is not dreaming in their world. The male psychiatrist tells him that his dreams are a way to avoid the pain of the loved one who has died. The other (a female) is intrigued by the problem-solving potential of his dreams.

The very fact that *Awake* is being broadcast on prime-time television intrigues me. The popularity of this show indicates a shift in mainstream attention to dreams. In 2010, a blockbuster movie called *Inception* took the media by storm. As soon as it appeared in the movie theaters, it seemed that every major newspaper or television newscast had a story about it. There was an article in the *Wall Street Journal*; CNN did a news story; NBC's *Today Show* featured it. Many mass media outlets interviewed experts about dreams, lucid dreaming (being aware that you are dreaming while you are dreaming) and mutual dreaming. The reporters were curious to find out if it is possible to "incept" ideas in another person's dreams.

When I started studying metaphysics in 1979, the media would not have been asking those questions. Dreams were relegated to the field of psychology and the hard news reporters considered dreams to be a "fluff" subject. To me, that seems odd, since we all dream. Not everybody remembers their dreams, but dreaming is a universal experience. So understanding what dreams are, why we dream, and how we can use them, seems to be an important endeavor for understanding who we are.

Multi-Dimensional Consciousness

Dreams can give us guidance. Once interpreted, they can tell us about our soul's needs, our own attitudes, and inform us about our state of awareness. In addition to this personal use of dreams, they can awaken us to the greater reality that extends beyond the brain and the conscious mind. Dreams can reveal ancient knowledge, help us to find lost objects, inspire artistic creation and scientific discovery.

> *Dreams can reveal ancient knowledge, help us to find lost objects, inspire artistic creation and scientific discovery.*

Dreaming is an actual experience in the subconscious mind. In the language of the School of Metaphysics, the word "mind" refers to the spirit, the soul, the psyche, and the conscious mind. The whole mind has three divisions. Superconscious mind, which you might call your inner divinity, is the closest to the core of who we are, Light. In the middle is the subconscious mind, where we dream, and the outermost division is the conscious mind. (See diagram of *Mind and Consciousness* p. 3.)

The conscious mind is where we exist when we are awake. It is the part of the mind that works with the body, the brain, and the physical senses. This is the part of the mind where we reason and make decisions. It is also where we imagine or envision our future, our hopes, and our limitations.

The brain is a physical organ. It is a part of the body and, as such, is something temporary. When the body dies, the brain dies. The mind is much larger than that. One reason why dreams fascinate people is that when we dream, we exist in the mind, or these inner levels of consciousness. The experience of dreaming gives people a taste of knowing that they are more than the brain and the physical body.

When you go to sleep at night, if you are in a deep state of sleep, your attention is not on your body. It is withdrawn from your brain and your physical senses. This is why you do not hear the phone if it rings. If the room is too hot, you do not feel it. In a shallow state of sleep, it might be different. You could incorporate the sound of the phone ringing into your dream. I once had an odd experience that demonstrates this phenomenon. I had fallen asleep on the couch taking a nap in a room with a huge picture window. All of a sudden I bolted awake (or so it seemed), because I thought a car had crashed through that glass window into the living room where I was sleeping. I heard the car horn so loudly it sounded like it was blasting right next to my ear.

I jumped up, and this time I really was awake, and with my physical ears I heard a car horn honking on a street six blocks away. What happened? When I first heard the car, thinking it had crashed into the building, I woke up in my dream, from a deeper state of sleep to a more shallow one. I was hearing in two dimensions, both with my physical ears and my mental sense or psi. When physical sounds enter the dreamstate they are often magnified, which is why the horn sounded so loud in my mind.

This dream within a dream occurred as I moved from one level of consciousness to another. The subconscious mind has four levels. The conscious mind only has one level, the physical level. We can dream in any level of consciousness, although most people remember dreams in the outer two levels of the subconscious mind.

Waking up within a dream is an experience of going into different levels of consciousness. When you think you have awakened and then find out that you are still asleep, sometimes you are going into a deeper state of sleep, or you may be bringing your dreaming attention more toward the surface, into a more shallow state.

That kind of experience is shown in the movie *Inception*. The characters think they have awakened, when they have actually moved into another level of mind. They wake up in a dream into a new dream scenario.

Some of the news stories or movie reviews described such

experiences as science fiction or fantasy. It is not. It can actually happen. You can exist in more than one level of consciousness and be aware of your existence in more than one level of consciousness. That is one way that dreams can awaken you to a greater perception of yourself.

You can also have the same dream as another person. In *Inception*, the characters have to be hooked up to a machine to induce mutual dreaming. Media people want to know, "Do we have the technology to be able to do this?" We do not need mechanical devices or drugs to accomplish that! The ability to exist in the same place in subconscious mind as other people is a natural function of the mind.

Dreaming opens the door to a greater reality than the physical existence. Have you ever had a dream of flying? Not in an airplane, but soaring through the air? Those are the best! People love flying dreams because there is a sensation of freedom and that freedom in the flying dream is who we really are. Often in waking life people feel trapped. They feel imprisoned by their jobs; sometimes they feel trapped by relationships that are not going well. They are bogged down by money problems. Although we may feel trapped by the experience, we are only restricted because we get stuck on our thinking.

Our real nature is freedom. In a flying dream, if you decide you want to go through the roof, all you have to do is picture the sky, and suddenly you are there! Or you decide that you want to go left, and as soon as you image yourself over there, voilá! There you are. We have that mental ability, to visualize and create our reality with thought.

In waking life, it doesn't usually happen so suddenly, in a moment, as it does in a dream, although every once in awhile we see, or hear about instant manifestation. There are stories of miraculous healing and people who can materialize objects purely by thinking. For most of us, it takes time for something to transform from thought to physical reality. Dreams can help us to become aware of our natural state of being so that we can learn how to become more conscious of how we think and create our lives.

Ancient Knowledge, Modern Application

Dreams can aid us live a more meaningful existence when awake. The subconscious and conscious minds work together in a kind of marriage. The conscious mind's duty is to think, to reason, and to produce understanding through our everyday life experiences. That is the purpose for living.

We are not here to make money, acquire things and entertain ourselves. We are here to produce understanding, like becoming more patient, or kind, or disciplined, developing qualities that make us more whole or holy. When the conscious mind is doing its duty to the subconscious mind by fulfilling those understandings, we experience peace, contentment, and security. When we live to be like our Creator, we may even feel bliss.

The subconscious mind's duty to the conscious mind is to fulfill our conscious desires. When there is something we want or need to understand, and we ask for guidance, the subconscious mind will give it to us.

Sometimes that guidance comes in the form of a dream. There are stories throughout history of inventors, scientists, statesmen, artists, musicians, entrepreneurs, all kinds of people who labored consciously to come up with solutions. When they had exhausted their conscious thinking, they turned to their dreams. You have probably heard people say, when they have worked a problem as far as they can go, "I need to sleep on it."

In drawing upon dream-wisdom, it is valuable to exercise the conscious mind first before turning the problem over to the subconscious mind. It is important to reason, to research, to think through whatever options or possibilities you have and then when you have reached the limit of your brain and conscious mind, to turn it over to your subconscious mind. The subconscious mind then can draw upon universal wisdom. It can weave things together in a way that consciously you might not know, allowing you to you receive intuitive insight.

Scientists and Inventors

Elias Howe invented the lock-stitch sewing machine. He was trying to figure out how to make a machine that could be used for sewing but could not figure out how to get the thread to make a reliable, regular stitch. As the story goes, a night-time dream gave him the detail he needed to produce a needle that was threaded at the point rather than the eye. Different written accounts describe Howe's dream in different ways. One account says he had a dream in which he was captured by cannibals who had these spears and were about to stab him. What he saw in his dream was that the spear had a round point at the very tip of the spear with a hole in it.[2] Another account reports that "Elias Howe told how the idea of a needle with a hole in the 'wrong end' came to him.

It was all a dream... Elias Howe was in the middle of a dream where Red Indians were attacking another Indian camp. They were shooting/firing arrows through wigwams made of stout cloth, not hide. As the arrows pierced the tents they snagged threads, drawing the threads through with the tips of the arrows creating large loops of loose thread. Elias woke in the middle of his dream, rushed to his workshop, and put his 'dream' into practice."[3]

This dream did not directly say to Mr. Howe, "OK, this is what you need for your sewing machine," but the visual imagery gave him the detail he needed. Sometimes that's how the dreams give answers.

Other famous dreamers include the chemist Kekule who discovered the ring-like structure of the benzene molecule when he dreamed of a snake with its tail in its mouth.[4] Sometimes the answers are a little more direct. After working for years to discover a pattern to the elements that make up atoms, Dmitri Mendeleyev dreamed the Periodic Table of Elements, "a table where all the elements fell into place as required."[5] One story says Mendeleyev had this dream when he fell asleep listening to his family playing chamber music.[6] Chamber music is a very structured type of music. In fact, research shows that the ordered rhythm harmonizes brain waves and helps the right and left brain work together. So perhaps this version is true!

Entrepreneurs

Some business leaders receive brilliant ideas from dreams. The first female Afro-American entrepreneur made her fortune from a dream-inspired idea. Mme. C.J. Walker was born to a family of share-croppers and her early years were fraught with poverty, abuse, and hardship. The stress of such a hard life caused her hair to fall out. She tried home-made remedies and doctor's treatments to no avail. Then, one night, she had a dream in which a "big Black man appeared to me and told me what to mix up for my hair. Some of the remedy was grown in Africa, but I sent for it, put it on my scalp, and in a few weeks my hair was coming in faster than it had ever fallen out."[7] The formula, "Madame C.J. Walker's Wonderful Hair Grower," worked for other people as well as herself, and by the early 1900's Mme. CJ Walker was a millionaire.

Jeff Taylor is another genius who founded the Monster Board, later to be known as Monster.com which was at one time the largest job search engine in the world. He had a dream of an electronic switchboard where people all over the world were plugging things in looking for jobs. In his dream he heard the words, "Monster board," so he woke up, wrote it down, and then went to a coffee shop and started scribbling down all of these ideas from which he invented Monster.com.

Artists, Musicians, and Writers

Since creative expression is closely linked to visual imagery, it seems natural that dreams can inspire art and music. Paul McCartney's famous song *Yesterday* is one example. He heard the music in his dream, and being a musician, had a piano in his room, so upon awakening he went over to the piano and played the tune. He wrote the notes on a musical score. As the story goes, along with the music, the lyrics that he heard in his mind were, "Scrambled eggs, how I love those luscious scrambled eggs." Obviously, those words would not sell too well, so he composed different lyrics for the song.

Whether this particular story is true or not, the fact is that sometimes the answers we receive from dreams have some useful components and some elements that still need to be worked out in the conscious mind. The marriage of the conscious and subconscious minds working together is essential to the creative process. It is not all one or the other.

Some famous writers have "dreamed up" images, ideas, or plots. Mary Shelley's **Frankenstein** , Stephen King's **Misery,** *Dr.* **Jekyll and Mr. Hyde** by Robert Louis Stevenson, and the poem *Kubla Kahn* by Samuel Coleridge were all inspired by dreams. One of the chapters in this book came from a dream, as did the art for the cover.

Battle Plans and Intrigues

Most people have read or heard of Custer's Last Stand. The history I studied when growing up said that General Custer and his troops were massacred by the Indians. Nobody mentioned that the white man was encroaching on the territory of the people who already lived there. Sitting Bull, who was a very wise ruler, wanted to cooperate with these new people. He did not want to fight. He wanted to be able to harmonize with the white men, and signed a treaty but it was short-lived.

The white settlers discovered gold in the Black Hills and wanted to take the land from Sitting Bull's people. They were ready to attack. Sitting Bull had a dream about the white men in bluecoats who were coming down from a cloud in the East. The dream alerted him to the direction from which Custer and his men were approaching. He responded to the prophecy, leading his people into the battle that saved them.

Caesar Augustus, a ruler who became an emperor of Rome, was also saved by a dream. When he was young, still called Octavian, a friend dreamed that he was going to be murdered in his bed. He actually was sick and wanted to sleep, but instead he arose and fled somewhere else. In the middle of the night soldiers came into his tent and stabbed his bed where they though he lay asleep. The bedclothes were ripped to shreds. Had he ignored his friend, Octavian would have been murdered. Because he listened to the dream, his life was spared.

Accessing your own dreams

Anyone, not just the people we learn about in legends, can draw upon the intuitive power of dreams. The next chapter gives examples of "ordinary" artists, entrepreneurs, and musicians whose dreams have inspired them. You, too, can open the door to your subconscious mind to discover treasures that may have previously been hidden from you.

Here are some simple steps that you can use to gain access to your own dreams so that you can draw upon their insight.

First, acquire a dream journal. Make it a special book to use just for your dreams and any notes or comments or interpretation. Put it by your bed before you go to sleep at night. Keep it by your side if you are going to take a nap, since sometimes the light sleep of napping is rich with dream insight. Date the dream journal for the next morning (if you are sleeping at night) and tell yourself, "I want to remember my dreams."

Dr. Deirdre Barrett, in a television interview on *The Today Show* about the movie *Inception*, said that half of dream-work is remembering your dreams. Dr. Barrett is a psychologist at Harvard University who has done extensive research on dreams, incubation, and creative problem-solving in dreams. Her book **The Committee of Sleep** is a well-known work detailing how dream incubation can be used to find answers.[8]

It is essential to remember dreams to be able to draw upon their insight. I think most of us have experienced waking up from a dream, remembering it, having the sense that it was very profound, and thinking, "Oh, I'll remember that dream!" so we don't write it down. Then, in a short time, sometimes as soon as we get out of bed, or by the end of the day or the end of the week, we do not remember it any more. Or we embellish it with imagined elements that were not in the original dream. This is why it is so important to write dreams down.

Recording your dreams allows you to capture the entire dream. Immediately upon awakening, the whole dream resonates in your mind. Even if at first the dream memory eludes you, try to lie there in bed with a quiet mind, holding your attention in the reverie state. Then write down the little bit that you do remember. You will soon find yourself remembering more and more until the rest of the dream unfolds. Discipline your mind so that you allow yourself to stay in the half-awake, half-asleep state as you bring your attention back to waking awareness. Do not start thinking about your upcoming day and your "to do" list until after you have recorded your dream.

Anyone can draw upon the intuitive power of dreams.

I have discovered many times that I record more in my dream notebook than I remember as I ponder the dream in the ensuing hours or days. Sometimes I write a dream down, and when I reflect on it throughout my day I think I am remembering the whole thing. But when, after a couple of days or a week, I go back to read what I wrote in my dream notebook, frequently my conscious remembrance was sparse compared to the detail I had written down. So the benefit of writing it is that you capture the whole dream. The more of the dream you remember, the more insight it is going to give you, especially if you are interpreting it symbolically.

Dream Incubation

If you want to incubate a dream, asking your dreams for a specific answer, it is very helpful before you go to sleep to write about the question that you are incubating. Let us say you are thinking about a change and you have considered moving to a new city, getting a different job, or being in a new environment.

Write a few pages in your journal about all of your thoughts concerning the move. Write in a stream of consciousness fashion where you do not stop and think about it; you just

let the pen move in your hand to express all of your thoughts.

Then draw a picture about your question. When you write, you engage your left brain. When you draw, you are engage your right brain. In terms of the mind, the writing engages the conscious mind and the drawing engages the subconscious mind. Then, in one sentence, state in a very clear form what you want to know from your dream.

Do not ask your dreams to make a decision for you. Do not ask a question like, "Should I move to Oregon?" The function of your subconscious mind is not to make decisions for you. You want to ask a more open-ended question like, "What is the learning opportunity if I move to Oregon?" or "What is the learning opportunity if I stay where I am?" or "What do I need to consider in terms of soul growth with a move?" Asking the right question is part of the art.

The science of dream incubation is the step-by-step process described in the last chapter. The art is deciding what question is going to direct your subconscious mind to the answer you are seeking, and then knowing how to interpret it. Even if you ask a question like, "Should I move?" and you get the answer, "yes," you might feel unsettled about it. That feeling occurs because you haven't established why you want to move or what moving could do for you. It is probably better to ask for understanding.

For example, when I incubate dreams for healing, I ask a question like, "What is this pain in my back telling me?" or "What do I need to understand from this illness?" I might ask, "What am I to learn from this pain?" and then ask for a healing to occur in the dream, or a healing message that I can apply when awake.

Building A Pathway

To establish a relationship with your own inner self, ask the question, write it down, and expect to receive an answer or insight. When you awaken, allow yourself to hold your attention still, keeping enough consciousness in your dream to recall what happened, and enough consciousness on your body to hold a pen and write down whatever you remember. Even if you think that you have not remembered the dream, write down something, because you might have a feeling, you might have a vague visual image, there might be a word. Sometimes writing down the fragment will jog your memory and you will recall more details. You might even remember the dream backwards, recording one scene and then remembering and writing, "before that" and "before that."

If you are certain that you have brought nothing back from your dream, then write down something in your dream notebook like, "It is getting easier and easier to remember my dreams." Or "Today I did not remember my dream but tomorrow I will!" In that way you are establishing a brain pathway, a habit, so that on subsequent mornings it becomes easier to remember your dreams. With a little bit of practice, the frequency and detail of your dream recall will increase.

Knowing that dreams are a valuable resource for solving problems and enhancing creativity can aid you to discover your inner genius. Whether you want money, inspiration, joy, or answers to everyday questions, dreams can bring you peace and security, aiding you to have greater meaning and purpose in your life.

Extraordinary Dreams from "Ordinary" People

Can everyone have extraordinary dreams? Yes! We all have psi experiences, although we may not identify them as such. Paying attention to the inner life enables us to recognize the "big dreams" that seem otherworldly. This chapter highlights a few such dreams from "ordinary" people. I put that in quotes because each person has a unique influence on everyone else. Many of these dreamers made life-changing decisions and have helped other people with their dream-inspired ideas.

There are artists and musicians, entrepreneurs and ministers, educators and innovators who share their stories here. I hope they stimulate you to become aware of your own intuitive dreams. You may have more than you realize! The subconscious mind fulfills our conscious desires, so ask your inner self to give you insight. When you keep a journal by your bed and ask yourself before sleep to remember your dreams, you will. Noticing meaningful coincidences when you are awake also opens your mind to recognize intuitive happenings. As you pay attention, your perception will increase.

Finding Your Calling

Many people wonder what to do with their lives. They want to discover their purpose or inner calling, the gift they are to give to the world. Jackie and Amy discovered their life work through dreams. They listened and acted on these dreams and now aid other people to discover their unique talents as well.

Jackie's story

Jackie Gaskins and her husband have four young daughters. She says, "A couple of years ago as I slept, I heard a story being told to me, word for word. I know this came from the Lord. As I slept I heard the words flowing from within my heart. I got up and decided to save it on my computer and did not have to think for one word. As my husband's alarm clock went off, I had finished.

The book was published last summer. It is called **The Four Princesses**. It is a children's book about four princesses who are each created with a gift/purpose to be used to help those that they come in contact with. When they use their gifts for the King, they bless those that they meet and change not only their lives but the community for the good.

This book has inspired me to start a nonprofit called Virtuous Girls for God, Inc. We started out as a group that helped young girls realize their gifts and purposes that God has given them. We teach and encourage them to use their gifts to love and bless all that they come in contact with to make a difference in their communities. We have now sponsored and are opening a youth/community center called The Remnant that will be used to reach out to all youth and people in the area. We want this to be a safe place where the love of the Lord is shared through outreach to those around us. We hope this is the first of many to come. God Bless."

— Jackie Gaskins, Director/Virtuous Girls for God, Inc."[1]

Amy's story

"Here is the background to my dream experience:

I was completely unhappy in my work as co-director of a non-profit organization, a spiritually conscious school. Although I loved the people and the school, I didn't like the work I was doing. I was only using about 10% of my potential and I felt called to so much more. Unfortunately, I didn't really know what that was.

As a Jill-of-all-Trades, I was skilled at web design/marketing, business administration and strategy, but was also an artist, spiritual counselor and interfaith minister. Trying to integrate everything felt impossible and whenever I chose one option over the others, I always felt out of alignment with myself and Spirit. Then I had a dream.

In the dream, I'm a bookkeeper, but instead of working with numbers in an office, I tend people's gardens.

I use my credit card to gather water from a spigot on the side of the house, water I know comes directly from Source.

Then I water people's lawns.

At the end of the day, I am standing reviewing the books while a disembodied male presence, who I experience as God, stands behind me.

*I notice I have a million dollars in **my** checking account. I feel I have made a mistake and accidentally put my clients' money in my account, but God points out that my clients all have a million dollars too, and that my million dollars is what I earned simply by helping other people.*

I am astonished that it is so easy to make money by helping people.

When I woke, I knew something remarkable had happened. For awhile I felt the dream may be urging me to go into bookkeeping, because that was one of my roles as co-director. But it didn't interest me, so I knew it was a metaphor for helping people earn an income.

After doing a series of creative exercises inspired by the dream, I started to have clarity. This clarity inspired me to quit my job without a plan.

Eight months later, I went from a nearly empty practice (few clients) to a full practice doing exactly what I loved doing.

The work I do is called "Grow Your Lifework." I've combined my skills and interests in a unique way to help women answer their calling and take their work into the world."

— Amy Brucker Grow Your Lifework: Inspired ideas that take your wisdom into the world[2]

Creative Inspiration

Because dreams come from the subconscious mind, they are a rich resource for creative inspiration. They can stimulate new ways of thinking. They give us fresh perspectives. We can tap dreams for answers when we reach the limits of our conscious thought processes.

pasQuale

pasQuale Ourtane-Krul is an avid and active lucid dreamer from the Netherlands. Her website LD4All provides education for beginners who want to learn how to become lucid dreamers. It serves as a networking community for experts who want to discuss their experiences with other lucid dreamers. pasQuale incubated dreams to help her develop the site. Her story can encourage people to foster creativity through drawing upon dream-guidance. You can read the entire history of the project development on the LD4All website.[3]

As Seen In My Dreams
  How I used my lucid dreams as a source of guidance and inspiration for the design of a website about lucid dreaming

"I'm the founder of LD4all.com, a website and community about lucid dreaming. Since the beginning in 1996 I have always used my lucid dreams as guidance and inspiration for the look of the website. I want to share with you two of the lucid dreams I have had which have profoundly influenced the graphics and layout of the website.

Uncovering a new creative flow
  In the early beginnings LD4all was called: 'Through the Mirror — Beyond Dreaming' and it was my graduation project

for Art School. In those days Internet was something new — so as a student in New Media I naturally felt drawn to the new medium. I decided to make a website about lucid dreaming. At that time, I had just discovered lucid dreaming myself, from reading the book **Creative Dreaming** by Patricia Garfield. I was so excited about it that I wanted to share this amazing ability with the world. And what better way to do it than a website."

pasQuale started to build the site but felt that "The site was boring. I got stuck. I didn't want to continue like that, but I also didn't know how to break out of my 'designer's block'. I decided to become lucid in a dream and search for the design of my project. I hoped to see something in my dream that would inspire me. That night, I became lucid.

I'm lucid and I'm standing in a hallway with doors on both sides. I remember wanting to dream of my project. So I say to myself: 'Behind this door I will see what my project will look like.' I open the door, step inside and there on a table sits a computer. I look at the screen and there I see what my project looks like.'"

Upon awakening, pasQuale sketched the images she received and used the dream-inspired vision to build the site. After graduating from college, she says, "I wanted my own domain name. 'throughthemirror.com' or something similar didn't have a ring to it so I had decided on a new name: LD4all. com. I really wanted a new look for my newly named website.

Once again, I decided to incubate a lucid dream to look for the design of the new LD4all. When I became lucid, I asked the dream to show me the new design for LD4all. The dream immediately responded. At first, I saw a huge golden logo, rotating in a starry sky. After the logo was shown, I saw an image of the layout of the website. When I woke up, I sketched all I could remember...

Before my lucid dream, I had already been working on the design of the logo, but no sketch I had made up to then really 'hit the mark.' Yet, I didn't really think of specifically looking for a logo in my dream, I just wanted to see 'the design.'

My lucid dream had presented me with the perfect logo. This was beyond any guidelines for design I had previously experienced in a lucid dream. The image of the huge golden logo, rotating in the starry sky stayed there for what seemed a long time, so I could really take in all details of it. But even though I knew exactly how it had to look, it was quite an effort to get it right. I had remembered the important elements: the way the 'beams' had to go over the surrounding border and the way the 'eye' was connected to the borders.

Above shows the sketch of the logo I made right after the dream. Next to it is the first official version of the logo, and the last image is the logo currently in use on LD4all.com.

Lucid dreams for inspiration

You have seen how I have used my lucid dreams as guidance for the design of my website. When I use my lucid dreams for inspiration, I always am surprised what the dream shows me. Even when I have sketched and drawn and thought about the design, the dream still comes up with something entirely different than I already have thought of when awake.

So if you ever have something you need inspiration for, why not use your lucid dreams for it? Call forth your project in your lucid dream and take a good look at it. Your dream could take you in new directions!"   — pasQuale Ourtane-Krul[4]

Dream-Inspired Writing

Most writers love it when ideas and metaphors seem to flow effortlessly through them. The painstaking work of trying to write, edit, and perfect a piece is quite a different experience! Dreaming can bring us inspiration. Just as the words to Jackie's story **The Four Princesses** were dictated in her sleep, the following authors found that their articles, poems, and plays have a life of their own when they come through dreams.

Roberta

"I'm a writer specializing in humor and frequently I write about the human-animal bond. Creative types ought to pay more attention to their dreams! Three different times I've dreamed full articles about cats.

Each time I woke up at my normal time, headed to my computer, and tried to recall enough of the dream to type phrases and key words. From there, it was a quick process. The words flowed easily and there was clearly a beginning, middle and end. Because I target print markets, I had to come up with an opening (lead) that wasn't part of the dream. No matter.

Dreams can spin magic! Only a single draft was necessary and I fooled around with the words a bit and sent the finished work out within an hour or so.

All sold to a national pet magazine. First editor. No rejections.

When I create an article from scratch, the process is much different. It's slower. I might start with a handwritten concept or a short list of some sort. At my computer, I try a few paragraphs, then set the work aside for a few days. When the time feels right, I revisit it and try to tweak it. I experiment with titles. Half these articles never get finished. They drift off halfway through and there's no sense in fighting it when there's nothing worthwhile happening."
                                    — Roberta Beach Jacobson[5]

Lindsay

Lindsay Vanhove is a creative artist and writer who receives images for her artwork and words that "puzzle automatically" into poetry in her dreams. She is from Belgium and although English is her third language, she sometimes dreams poetry in English. She writes the words down as soon as she awakens, even if it is 4 a.m.

Here are a few poems that came to her in dreams:

Our bodies
- Mixed together
Harmonized
- Gently lifted
I can remember
- The swirling tones
In every. Single. Fragment.
We breathe with colors.

Her pale blue eyes
Know more than we do
Her little hands grab mine
As she falls asleep.

You can reach for
The deep waters
And come back to life

I knew we'd stay
With holding hands
For there is no other who
Keeps the vision awake.

He watched the world
In total silence
And broke it with
One whispered word

"March..."
Meant for she who
Takes the spiral stairs

Taking his hand to travel
Entwined.

We don't talk
Out loud
Simply because we
Speak at night

My head on your
chest feels the rhythm
Of your words.
It's karma,
And all will be
Alright.

— Lindsay Vanhove[6]

Yaina

Yaina Cantrell is a social worker and life coach by day, but her passion is writing. She would love to be a full-time screenwriter. Yaina listens to her dreams because they aid her to create:

"Some of my best ideas have come to me in dreams. I keep a tape recorder on my bedside table for the purpose of capturing those inspirations before they fade away. It's funny how sometimes I can wake myself when I have an inspiring dream. That usually happens when I go to bed worried about a speed bump I've hit on a writing project. Some people call it writer's block. I don't like that terminology because it inhibits my process. So, I just call it a speed bump when there's something that I can't figure out. Many times my dreams have provided the solution and gotten me over those speed bumps, allowing me to finish the chapter, Third Act, or whatever I was stuck on."

Yaina's favorite story concerns a screenplay that came to her from a recurring dream:

"The recurring dream I mentioned to you led to my first screenplay *7 Lucys.* I was having this strange dream for five years almost every night. There was a young woman (sometimes it was me) who would be walking around outside, usually at night, through various scenarios. For instance, the dream would begin with 'Lucy' walking into a bar, and she'd be dressed for a night out on the town ... she'd be socializing with people, having a good time. Then, she would head for the bathroom; but when she opened the door, she would enter a whole different scenario, and her appearance would change accordingly. The woman in my dreams would never seem to notice these changes. She would just effortlessly blend in.

One day, I decided to write it down because it was like a really good movie playing in my head. I enjoyed these dreams, although sometimes (particularly when I was the woman) I would feel disturbed by some of the scenarios she/I walked into. A few of them were what I would call nightmares.

When I finally sat down to write the screenplay, I was so flooded with images and memories of that dream, that it took only one month to complete!"

As Yaina reflected on the dreams that inspired the screenplay, she remembered a detail that stimulated her to consider writing a sequel to the original play:

"I stopped having that dream a couple of years before I wrote it down. Oddly, the dreams stopped when a man started to appear, stalking her, chasing her from one scenario to the next. He wasn't a menacing presence. He was more searching for her, and I remember feeling his longing and desperation. When he found her and confronted her, he told her that she had been lost and tried to remind her of who she was. Soon after, I lost the dreams. I had a few more dreams in which the two of them seemed to fall in love. I was her in one of those dreams, and I felt like I had been rescued by the man. So now, I'm thinking about writing another screenplay, a more pure version of my dream. *7 Lucys* is kind of a dark take on my dreams. I'm in a different place now, mentally & spiritually; so I'm seeing a whole new movie unfolding."
— Yaina Cantrell[7]

Yaina's experience brings to light one of the benefits of recording our dreams and writing the story in an objective fashion. It aids us to see ourselves more objectively, allowing us to write new stories for our waking lives.

Composing Music

Handel's Messiah and Paul McCartney's song *"Yesterday"* are two well-known pieces of music their composers heard in dreams. Capturing dream music and writing it down may be challenging. Some dreamers keep a voice recorder by the bed to sing or hum the tunes they hear in dreams. Modern technology also gives us computer programs and synthesizers that can reproduce the music one hears in the mind.

Curtiss

Curtiss Hoffman is a brilliant man who is accomplished in many areas of life. An archeologist and consciousness researcher in the Department of Anthropology at Bridgewater State College, he is particularly interested in cultural systems of thought related to dreaming, myth, ritual, visions, religious iconography, and symbolism.

A long-time member active on the Board of IASD, Curtiss is an avid dreamer. Although not a musician by profession, he composed a cantata that came through his dreams, unfolding as he studied Jung's **Red Book**. This story is an excerpt from an article in *Dream Network Journal*.

"As I reported in *Dream Network Journal* Vol. 29 #3, during the summer of 2010 I read Jung's **Red Book** and it had a profound effect upon my consciousness. Themes from the book frequently appeared in my dreams... The 'biggest' dream in this series concerned my observation of a group of choristers performing an *a capella* cantata based upon texts from the **Red Book**. Upon awakening, I realized that the texts derived from the 'Incantations' section of the book, in which Jung presents a series of prayers within his dreaming that was directed to the Babylonian hero Gilgamesh...

Subsequent dreaming has made it clear to me that I have been asked to compose this cantata out of themes my dreaming presents to me. Even though I had no formal education in musical composition, I agreed to undertake this project. The first stage was to translate the words of the Incantations from German into Akkadian, the actual language of the Gilgamesh epic. My training in ancient Near Eastern languages has made it possible for me to accomplish this. Next, I am applying to the Incantations section text the specific musical themes derived from my dreams.

My dreams indicated that the cantata would be sung *a capella* by four voices, and that it would be in six sections. In order to manifest this, I have audited two Music Theory courses this year, which enabled me to set the melodies my dreams gave me within a tonal harmonic structure. Far from easy!

The first section I was moved to set to music is associated with a powerful **Red Book** image (Jung 2009:55): the sun barque of the Egyptian god Ra sailing over the surface of the waters, beneath which lurks a monstrous fish, identified by Jung as the 'Spirit of the Depths.' The text consists of four lines and the melody for it was given to me in a dream. Translated into English, these are:

> *One word, which has never yet been spoken*
> *One light, which has not yet shone*
> *One confusion, without equal*
> *And one road, without end.*

Underlying the text, the Akkadian words for 'Spirit of the Depths' are intoned as an undulating pedal, representing the waves. In addition, singers from time to time hold long notes on "a," which is the Sumerian word for water.

The piece is in four sections, each of which corresponds to one of the four lines of the text...

This piece was premiered at the 2011 IASD Conference to a receptive audience. A second section of the cantata was performed in August of 2011 at the same music camp that provided the inspiration for the original dream that 'commissioned' the cantata.

Since I undertook the writing of the cantata, dreams about it have come in profusion. I have had 47 dreams in which the cantata was featured, 35 providing musical themes. In 11 of these, I have actually visualized the notes on the staff; more often, I just hear the themes. Most of these dreams are just brief snippets... or the theme occurs only at the end of a longer dream. Some dreams have provided me with insights into the structure of the cantata or helped me to revise what I have written. I know that there are themes that I have not been able to recall in the morning, but one dream early in the process informed me that these are being stored in my unconscious for when I will need them later on.

The creative process sometimes takes unexpected twists and turns... As Jung observed of the paintings which accompany his dreams in the **Red Book**, sometimes they didn't come out the way he expected! In many instances, I have no idea with what portion of the cantata the themes will go. But in other cases, I get the words with the music. My knowledge of music enables me to see that some of the themes bear a relationship to existing music. But other themes are unfamiliar and hopefully my dreams will give me more!"

— Curtiss Hoffman, "The Gilgamesh Cantata:
A Personal Exploration of Dreams and Music"[8]

You can hear pieces from the cantata sung by the Bridgewater State chamber choir on YouTube. There is also a computerized audiofile on the digital version of the *Dream Network Journal* Winter 2011.

Sean

Sean's experience was a bit different. He composed a song that he heard telepathically while his friend slept. His story shows how connected we can be mentally, whether awake or asleep.

"Perhaps seven months ago I had an extra roommate in a very small cabin in Pasadena. For him life was hectic, a series of unfortunate events, though he did expend considerable effort developing extrasensory faculties, especially through dreaming. He had just re-read the writings of Carlos Castandeda about Don Juan, and was practicing lucid dreaming frequently.

On one particular night, I had been working late and was in quite an exhausted, albeit cerebral state. I came home and found him passed out on the couch, sleeping serenely. Something struck me about Alex at that moment, and I felt compelled to pick up my guitar. I plugged in and simply sat holding my Gibson SG for a while ... listening to the silence. All of a sudden, without fiddling around, testing guitar chords, or practicing any fingering, a new, unique, melodious, and truly lovely song came out of my heart and through my fingers. It was definitive, and simply needed words.

The next morning, I woke up incredibly excited. "Alex!" I said. "I know this might sound weird, but last night I wrote the music to a song while watching you sleep. I want you to hear it." Not only was he unsurprised, but curious to see if it was what he thought it was. I played the new music.

"Oh my God!" he said, "That's it!"

"What?" I asked. He went on to explain his first love, how he had written the words to a song for her. It was called 'To Lauren'. But he was not a very skilled musician, and could never actualize the music that he heard in his head. That night when I found him, he had been dreaming of Lauren, the words to his poem cycling through his head. When I played the music, he was floored, because that was the fitting music he had swirling elusively in his mind for years.

He rifled around through his things (he was more or less homeless, and had the messy collection of his belongings behind the couch). Finally he comes up with a composition notebook, finds the appropriate page, reads for a minute, and says, "Okay. Play it again". He wasn't kidding, the pieces fit, and even today, its one of my favorite songs."

— Sean Skelton

Artistic Inspiration

Since dreams communicate in images and metaphors, it seems natural for artists to draw upon the imagery for their art. Gay Foltz has a great story to tell about a dream that changed the way she creates.

Gay

"I am a professional woodcarver and a vivid dreamer.

I had a dream where I went to England and came upon a little shop where a woman sold her woodcarvings. I really liked the carvings even though the faces weren't pretty. I bought a bunch of them and planned on shipping them home as gifts.

When I woke I grabbed my sketch tablet and drew some of the carvings that I bought in the dream. I have incorporated the look of these figures in some of my carvings. Then I worried that I was infringing on the copyright of the woman in my dream!

I have many dreams but this is one I've actually used in my work.

The carvings I've done using the images from the dream have sold very well. It has been a different direction for me and of course some people like the stuff I was doing before better. I'm having a lot of fun with the new stuff, it has taken me out of the rut I felt I was in." — Gay Foltz, Village Artisans Gallery[9]

Messages from Beyond

As we have seen in previous chapters, people who have died can come to us in our dreams because physical death means a change of form, not annihilation. The spirits of those who have passed on watch over us. They can communicate while we are awake or asleep. Many people find it easier to receive such messages in dreams, because during sleep the conscious mind limitations and chatter cease to interfere. Our minds are more attuned to the ethereal vibrations.

Laura A.

Laura Atkinson is an artist who creates in a number of media. Her favorite is photography. Laura's photo of the **Bible** with the heart appears in the "Inner Level Communication" chapter. This black-and-white book cannot do justice to her breathtaking photographs, so go to Laura Nova Photography to see for yourself "the colors of simplicity" she describes here!

Laura had a dream that she titled, "Many messages within the same dream." The dream starts out with a woman who wants to make a change, and ends with this scene that gave Laura a message that changed the way she approaches photography. It changed her life, bringing her great joy. The dream message came from a woman named May Tung, who was a member of the IASD and the World Dreams Peace Bridge.[10] May passed away in 2006. From time to time, members of the Bridge have dreams in which May appears with transcendent advice.

Here is the final scene of the dream in which May appears.

Laura writes,

A Chinese woman with gentle but masculine energy comes between H. and me and grabs our hands. This woman looks like May Tung, or what I imagine what she must have looked like in her early 20s. She says that she was once an artist and tells us the secret to her inspiration. "Look for small patterns of beauty in every moment, the way his hand holds yours, the pattern of your dress, the taste of the tea that you drink. Be overwhelmed with the colors of simplicity."
— Laura Atkinson, Laura Nova Photography[11]

Laura P.

Laura Pallatin received a similar message that inspired her to write a book about spirit communication.

"While I've had a few paintings come into my mind while I was dreaming, and heard music in dreams that I've never heard before, the most dramatic experience I've had involved my step-mom who has passed away. It was a very lucid dream which seemed more real-time and vivid than a normal dream.

My step-mom, Alice, and I were on a train looking out a window together as the world passed by. She put her arm around me and leaned in and said, 'Remember to treasure every moment of your life.' I leaned over to give her a hug and when I looked out the window again, I found myself looking out my bedroom window right next to my bed instead. I was still dreaming and Alice told me that it was time to lie down next to my 'beloved.' I felt myself float up in the air and gently re-enter my sleeping body.

The instant I was fully in my body I opened my eyes. I felt wonderfully blessed by the experience. It was profound and I used her quote in my book, *Walk In Your Own Footsteps.*"

— Laura Pallatin[12]

Tracey

Tracey Erikson is a student and volunteer teacher at the School of Metaphysics, a mother and wife, and works full time. Her grandmother appeared to her in a dream that four years later resonates in her consciousness:

"I had a dream that is still on my mind from fall 2008. I found the School of Metaphysics shortly after this dream. My grandma died a few years before I had this dream. Here it is:

I was in a very crowded place, it was a big room, and it reminded me of Grand Central Station or something like that. At first I could see all the people around and hear all the hustle-bustle, the color was very bright and flowing with the people. My Grandma showed up in front of me, and suddenly it was like we were on a stage because the people weren't around us anymore. We were raised slightly above them. (The other people were kind of blurry, like at that point it was only background. I felt like it was a way for my attention to be only on my Grandma.) The 'stage' had a bright red background, like a huge flag was hanging or something. I was so happy to see her; I asked how she has been and what she has been doing. All she said was 'I've been trying to get the Lord on your side.' Then I awoke, crying, actually sobbing uncontrollably.

My husband Neil woke up too, and he couldn't comfort me. I thought that the dream meant that I was on my way to hell or something. I thought, 'What! The Lord is not on my side??' So I couldn't stop thinking about the dream, it was a core-shaker."

Tracey reported that she had this dream at a pivotal time in her life. She had learned about the School of Metaphysics from a co-worker when they were taking a cigarette break at work. Tracey says, "She kept telling me that I would love the school and it seemed like a good place for me. She ended up giving me the little yellow **Concentration** book. I put the book in my desk drawer and went on with my life. About a year or more passed and we were moving our desks around at work, so I cleaned out my desk and found that little book. I took it out and read it and when I got to the end of the book it talks about the school and it really did sound interesting coming from someone experienced with Metaphysics. I found that book at just the right time in my life, because had I read it when B. gave it to me, it just wouldn't have clicked the same way it did. I called the school branch in Des Moines immediately."

Tracey became a student and teacher at the School of Metaphysics, learned how to meditate, developed her prayer life, and has become much more concentrated and purposeful. She uses what she is learning and work and to teach her young children to be more centered and focused.

She asked me how I would interpret the dream because four years later it still puzzled her. I said that symbolically, I understand that Grandma symbolizes superconscious mind or High Self and the big room in the dream is probably universal mind because of the presence of all the different people. A train station indicates awareness of a group or organization because a large vehicle like a train takes you somewhere in life ... so it makes sense that this dream was a precursor to Tracey becoming a student at SOM.

If it were my dream, I would receive it as a sign that my superconscious mind was trying to get through to me. I would heed the message from Grandma and act on the desire to align with the Lord, my own I AM. The urgency to know God and align with superconsciousness was very strong at the time. Nothing else was more important, which is why the other people faded away and the dreamer could only see and hear Grandma who was elevated. Tracey wanted to know why she woke up crying. I told her that if it were my dream, the emotion would be telling me to listen to superconscious mind and align with my Divine Plan ... that it was the most important thing! Walking a different path was causing pain. Tracey said that made sense to her and she was glad that the dream got her attention so that she could make some important changes in her life.

Sometimes visitation dreams have messages not so life-changing but nonetheless truthful and helpful. Lottie and Maria had dreams in which loved ones from the "other side" helped them to find lost objects. These experiences affirmed that they were not alone and that they could still connect with their relatives if they listened to their dreams.

Lottie

Pat tells the story of her Aunt Lottie, an eccentric woman who lived to an advanced age. After her brother Chester died, Lottie continued to live in the house that they had shared. In the later years of her life, sometimes Lottie's subconscious (inner) reality entered into waking reality. Some people called her senile, although she was a highly intelligent woman who often saw and knew things that people around her ignored. Some of her family passed her off as a bit crazy but this dream proved otherwise.

Aunt Lottie could not find her glasses and looked for them everywhere. After searching for quite awhile, Chester appeared in a dream, showing her where they were, in an obscure spot in the basement. Lottie suffered from arthritis and it was difficult for her to walk down the stairs to the basement to fetch them. She also could not see very well in the dim light without her glasses. She told people about the dream, asking them to look for her glasses, but they thought she was just making it up and ignored her.

Finally, one of her relatives decided to humor her and went to look in the place that Chester showed her in the dream. Lo and behold, there were Aunt Lottie's missing glasses! I  wonder who was more centered in "reality" ... Aunt Lottie or those who thought she was crazy?

Maria

Maria's friend Christine, who is a teacher at the School of Metaphysics, reports this dream that Maria told her.

"A few years ago I met up with Maria, a friend from college, and we talked about dreams and metaphysics. She said the night that her grandmother died she had a dream and her grandmother came to her and told her where to find her (the grandmother's) wedding ring. It was hidden in an unusual place and her grandmother showed her in the dream where to look. The most unusual part of this was that her grandmother died during the night and Maria did not know she had passed until the next morning. The dream was quite vivid to her. A few days later, when no one could find the said wedding ring, Maria quietly went to her grandmother's house and looked under dishtowels in the bottom drawer in the kitchen. She found the ring!

I could tell this dream experience was amazing to Maria, she didn't understand how something like that could happen, she only knew that it *did* happen.

I love dream experiences like this because they are undeniable to the dreamer and sometimes it is what motivates the person to delve more deeply into the meaning of all of their dreams."

How You Can Draw Upon the Inspiration in Your Own Dreams

Many of these dreamers' accounts show the importance of capturing the dream memory immediately upon awakening. Whether you keep a dream journal or have an audio recorder by your bedside, it is important to record the dream as soon as you wake up.

Once you have voiced, or written, or sketched your dream, you can decide how to use its message. As you have read, many of these dreamers needed to work with the dream by applying the message consciously.

Paying attention to your waking experiences is very helpful for developing the skill needed to pay attention to dreams. It is a good practice to become a critical, clinical observer in your waking life. Be purposeful. For example, when you are walking or driving, notice the street signs as you pass them. Say the names of the streets out loud. When you are introduced to new people, pay attention to their facial features, what they are wearing, how their voice sounds, and say their name out loud.

You can become aware of your environment by looking for something new every time you walk into a room, or your place of work, or a restaurant that you frequent. This keeps you from taking for granted the places with which you are familiar.

Give attention to your senses. Practice describing how your food tastes, the textures of the clothing you wear, the scent and colors of the plants you walk by, the sounds of the birds and wind and city noises.

Any of these practices will aid you to observe more carefully. By developing this acumen when awake, you will be able to bring it into your dreams.

It can also be helpful to read your dream journal before you go to bed, to read literature about dreaming or creativity, to draw or look at images that to you seem dreamlike. When someone wants to become a writer, he or she is advised to read other writers. Artists study other artists. The Grand Ultimate Principle in Feng Shui states that when you give attention to something each day it grows. To become more attuned to intuition and creativity in your dreams, give it attention every day.

Share your intuitive and creative dream experiences with others. You might be an inspiration to other people as I hope these dreamers have been for you!

Day Residue:
Should we pay attention?

"I dreamed I was at work, and my boss was telling us that there were pending layoffs in the company, just like he told us yesterday."

"I dreamed I kept seeing the computer screen with the data I'd be entering all day."

"All night long I was dreaming about the hailstorm that battered my car yesterday."

"I kept dreaming of that movie I saw last night. The same scene kept appearing over and over."

Many people dream of events that occurred during the day. Sometimes the dream seems to be simply a re-play of the day's happenings, with no change or embellishment. This is known as "day residue."

Day residue is a term that comes from Freud. It means dreaming of images or experiences from the previous day's activities. The word "residue" has interesting connotations. Defined as "remains" or "what is left over," residue often implies junk. For example, the online Merriam-Webster dictionary uses these sentences as examples of the word *residue:*

The grill was covered in a greasy residue from the steak.
The divorce left a residue of pain in the family.
There was some kind of sticky residue on the floor.

Because people associate residue with something unwanted or unpleasant, they question the relevance of day residue in dreams. Are these images from the day interfering with the dream message? Do they get in the way of the "real" dream that our subconscious mind wants us to receive? Or is this something that warrants our attention? Could the day residue be communicating important knowledge to the dreamer?

From a metaphysical perspective, I understand dreams as an experience of consciousness. They reflect the dreamer's state of awareness. The events of the day also reflect the dreamer's state of awareness. In other words, people create the kind of waking experiences they have with their thoughts, attitudes, and choices. Even when people are not solely responsible for causing physical events, their perception determines how they interpret the quality and meaning of these happenings in the physical world.

For example, some years ago, I was giving a presentation to a group of social workers in Cincinnati, Ohio. It was in early September. There had been a long spell of hot, dry weather throughout July and August. The workshop took place during the day in a downtown office building. When it was over, at 4 o'clock in the afternoon, I came down the elevator, walked out of the building and found, to my surprise, that it was raining hard. I waited in the doorway of the building while my companion went to get our car that was parked several blocks away.

As I waited, I witnessed two people react to the rain in completely different ways. The first was a woman, dressed in a business suit. She had carefully coiffed hair, high heels, and was carrying an expensive briefcase. She walked out of the building, saw the rain, frowned, and complained, "The weather in Cincinnati is always horrible!" Then, she crossed her arms protectively around her briefcase and minced her way down the block.

Minutes later, a man came out of the building. When he saw the rain, he drew in a deep breath, inhaling the fresh air, and exhaled completely with a delighted, "Ahhh!" He said, "Don't you love it? The rain! We've been waiting for this for a long time!" Although he was also dressed in business attire, he walked out onto the sidewalk with his arms outstretched, face to the sky as if to catch the raindrops, and then sprinted across the street.

Two people reacted to the same event in contrasting ways because of their unique outlooks. The happening was neutral: rain in early September in downtown Cincinnati. Yet, the disparity in attitude and mindset produced a different experience for this man and woman.

What does this tell us about life, and by extension, our night-time dreams? We might consider life to be like a schoolroom. We go through our daily lives to learn, to grow, to develop, and progress spiritually. Dreams can give us feedback about our attitudes. They can guide us, informing us regarding the lessons we are learning, or need to learn, in this waking existence. French Jesuit priest and philosopher Pierre Teilhard de Chardin wrote in *The Phenomenon of Man*, "We are not human beings having a spiritual experience; we are spiritual beings having a human experience."

In this light, dreams are not *about* physical events. The dream is always about the Self. *How* that dream is communicated is the subject of this chapter.

Where Do Dreams Originate?

The subconscious mind, or inner self, is like a best friend that wants to aid us in our soul progression. It wants to fulfill our desire to learn. It can reach out to draw to us what we need for our soul progression, using any available resources to communicate with us.

Dreaming is one means the inner mind uses to facilitate our growth. In dreams, the subconscious mind can tell us what we need. The conscious mind needs to listen to hear the message that our inner self wants to get across. The subconscious mind uses anything it can find to give us that which we seek. When it wants to tell or show us something, it draws upon the images and information in the dreamer's brain. Images from the recent day's experiences are readily accessible, so the dreaming mind may use those images to express itself.

During the day, when we are awake, the conscious mind gathers information through the physical senses and the mental sense of attention. When alert, we learn by giving our attention to the outward world, interpreting the "input" received in the brain according to our point of view. In the example I just related, the man and woman both gathered information about the weather through the senses of sight, touch, and smell.

The difference in their interpretation of "rain in downtown Cincinnati" came from their disparate vantage points. One viewed the rain with displeasure and the other was pleased by it. Their different perspectives may have been influenced by related memories or by imagined outcomes. Both people gave attention to the present conditions and then added their judgment and opinion. "I'm cold. I just paid to get this suit cleaned. I can't run in these high heels. I'm going to ruin my briefcase," in the woman's mind or "I love the smell of the air when it rains. How refreshing this is after being cooped up in a stuffy office all day. I am so glad my garden is getting watered. I can't wait to get home and play in the rain with my kids."

As Shakespeare said, "Nothing is either good or bad but thinking makes it so." If we could discover how to improve the quality of life, wouldn't we seek a way to do so? Dreams can help. They can give us feedback on our waking attitudes. Interpreting dreams can tell us how we interpret the day-to-day waking reality we call "life." The subconscious mind has access to the information we have stored through our senses and attention, and it may weave these images together into a thought-form we experience during sleep as a dream.

In Hindu teachings, mind stuff or mind substance is known as "akasha." When a waking thought, or a dreaming thought, impinges on the mind substance, it is called a "vritti." You might consider waking thoughts and dreams to be like ripples in the waters of consciousness. The self, whether the awake thinker or the sleeping dreamer, is the one who understands their meaning and purpose.

The practice of concentration to still the mind so that it becomes calm, like a pool of water without any waves, enables us to accurately receive impressions and interpret them without prejudice. As noted above, the vibration itself is neutral. The attitude of the individual determines whether we view it as pleasant or unpleasant, meaningful or chaotic. Some people report that seemingly supernatural or paranormal dreams are fun and inspire further discovery. Others are afraid of such dreams, finding them scary because they upset their pre-conceived ideas about reality.

My perspective on psi dreams is the former. I enjoy dreaming with other people, recognizing telepathic connections both while awake and while asleep. It enriches my life to develop such multi-dimensional relationships. When I look at my life and experiences as a laboratory in which I am the scientist who studies my Self, the discovery process is energizing and sometimes entertaining.

In this chapter I will describe two experiences I had with purposeful intuitive dreaming. Both of these arose during the International Association for the Study of Dreams (IASD)'s online PsiberDreaming Conference, giving me direct knowledge of the connection between day residue and psi dreams.

The PsiberDreaming Conference is an online dream conference sponsored by the International Association for the Study of Dreams. People from all over the globe participate, creating an intensive force-field of dreamers who are connected both online and in the dreamtime for two weeks. My ability to dream with other people has increased remarkably during the PsiberDreaming Conference because of the concentrated focus on dreams, writing, poetry, and imagery. (There is an Outer Inn, a virtual inn for playing with creative ideas and interchanges with other people. This creative playground lends itself to the free-flowing kind of expression that enhances dream imagery.)

Now that the internet enables us to make virtual connections with people around the globe, we can "meet" people online and dream with those people even when we have never seen them in the flesh. This seems to increase the awareness of our mental influence and intuitive connections with one another.

When I attended the IASD Annual Conference in 2010 in the Netherlands, I met people in person for the first time — from Spain, Germany, Sweden, Belgium, Norway and other countries — whom I had previously only met online at the PsiberDreaming Conferences.

What is "Psi Dreaming"?

The Parapsychological Association defines "psi" as "a neutral term for parapsychological phenomena, inclusive of both ESP and mind-matter interaction."[1] Psi is the 23rd letter of the Greek alphabet and first letter of the word "psyche." I would define psi as the mind or consciousness, and a psi dream as an experience in the inner levels of consciousness. Most people describe so-called paranormal dreams as psi dreams. Mutual dreaming, dream telepathy, visitations, clairvoyant or precognitive dreams, and dreaming of past lives, are all examples of psi dreams. When we sleep, we go into the subconscious mind. Some people find that it can be easier to draw upon intuition in the dream state than in the waking state when the conscious mind and conscious ego exert greater control.

For example, a visitation dream in which someone who has died comes to you can be an actual meeting with that spirit who no longer lives in a physical body. Other people may think that such an occurrence is the dreamer's memory of the person who has died, or their conscious thoughts or emotions about it. (Most dreamers who have had such experiences have no doubt that the visitation was an actual meeting with the deceased loved one.) From my perspective, a person who has died can actually come to you in the dreamtime to give you a message or simply to be with you. You can also have mutual dreams with people who are still alive. Mutual dreaming seems to happen frequently at dream conferences when people are together during the day immersing themselves in dream-knowledge and practice, and then at night they continue these interactions in their dreams.

How do we know when a dream is purely symbolic and when it is one of these psi dreams? Experience, trust, and practice are the best ways I know to develop this kind of discernment. One thing I love about the IASD is that people enjoy learning together, playing games, exploring creative ways to understand their own minds, learning about their own intuition. Dream contests are one method of practicing these skills.

Intuitive Dream Contests

The PsiberDreaming Conference includes experimenting with psi phenomena through contests. These intuitive dream contests also take place at the in-person conferences, they may seem easier to practice in one's own bed at home. (Curtiss Hoffman jokes that with so many activities that extend into the wee hours of the morning, the nickname for IASD at these in-person annual conferences is the International Association for Sleep Deprivation!) Some people find that their dream recall diminishes as the conference progresses because they are sleeping for shorter periods of time.

During the PsiberDreaming Conference at designated times on specific days there are dream tasks for anyone who wants to participate, testing his or her skill with precognition, telepathy, and mutual dreaming.

The challenge is to evaluate one's own experience, record and report the dreams, and to trust oneself in identifying which elements of the dream one considers to be the psi content (as distinguished from the rest of the dream.) To add to the fun, people donate prizes such as books they have written on dreams, homemade crafts, CDs or DVDs on dream-related subjects, and other magical objects.

During the contests, there are discussion threads for participants to write about their experiences, and to learn from the more seasoned intuitive dreamers such as Drs. Robert van de Castle, Ed Kellogg, Robert Waggoner, Rita Dwyer, and others. It is an open environment for learning and discovery.

On two occasions, once with the dream telepathy contest and once with the mutual dreaming contest, I had dreams that I thought were just day residue. I was frustrated and kept trying to get those images out of my mind because I thought that they were interfering with the intuitive nature of the dreams. However, despite my denial, I was willing to put myself on the line and report what I saw in my dreams. To my surprise, one of these dreams won a fourth place, and the other one won an honorable mention. As it turned out, what I thought was "just" day residue actually communicated psi information.

Clearing the Mind

To prepare for the psi dreaming contests, the first instruction is to clear the mind of day residue. Ed Kellogg, who directs the Phenomenological Laboratory in Ashland, Oregon and who has indexed over 30,000 of his own dreams, has explored lucid dreaming and consciousness for well over 30 years. He believes that one's own experience is the best way to know truth. (He has written extensively on the topic of developing psi abilitites and lucid dreaming. You can learn more by reading his papers published online: http://dreamtalk.hypermart.net/member/files/ed_kellogg.html). He initiated these contests to encourage the development of self-observation and self-evaluation, to strengthen one's own knowing of intuition in dreams. To prepare for the contests, Dr. Kellogg describes a step-by-step description of how to clear the mind. He calls it "clearing the stage." This is to sweep the mind clean of any type of noise, chatter, or interference.

To illustrate the importance of this practice, the following story shows how unaware we may be of the clutter in our own minds. Some years ago, I attended a conference in Puerto Rico sponsored by an organization called the Alliance for a New Humanity. The Alliance's mission is to connect and inspire people who, through personal and social transformation, are leading a conscious evolution toward a more peaceful and compassionate world.

The second night of the conference, I found myself lying in bed, physically tired but mentally alert, trying to go to sleep and irritated with myself because my mind was racing. The conference started early in the morning and ran until late at night, and I knew I needed to rest so that I could be refreshed for the next day. But I couldn't get my thoughts to stop buzzing around, keeping me awake. I decided to exercise some mental discipline to quiet my mind.

At the School of Metaphysics, we teach our students an

exercise called a 5-day, 5-step reversal. It is designed to clear the conscious mind by remembering five events backwards for five days backwards. It is somewhat like a slide show in reverse. You clear your mind of all of the unfinished business, memories, or thoughts upon which you are dwelling. Doing a flashback in a controlled manner serves the purpose of sorting through the images from recent memory and filing them where they belong. You might liken it to clearing your desk by looking at the papers on the desktop and putting them in the appropriate place in the file cabinet.

When I couldn't fall asleep at the end of my conference day, I did this 5-day, 5-step reversal exercise, and when my mind became quiet, I actually listened to the thoughts that were causing the noise. They were voices in Spanish, and I don't speak Spanish! At that moment, I realized that it was not my own thoughts that were distracting me. I was receiving telepathically the thoughts of people in the hotel. Puerto Rico, and especially this particular hotel on the beach, is quite a "party place." People stay up all night long, dancing and entertaining. So the noise was, indeed, mental noise, but it was not my own. It was as if I had tuned into an old-fashioned telephone party line or had left a radio on and was hearing the unwanted broadcast.

Once I recognized what was happening, I could relax rather than being so angry with myself for having such a busy brain. I was able to remove my attention from the voices in my mind and focus it upon my desire for sleep. I imaged myself slipping into a sweet, quiet place. Upon relaxing, I was able to fall asleep and slept for a short but restful period of time.

This example shows how essential it is to clear the mind of extraneous thoughts, noise, images, and impressions to become aware of what is occurring in one's own mind.

Observe, Report, and Describe

The next instruction in the psi dreaming instructions is to describe your dream with the scenes, the characters, the emotions and the events. At the School of Metaphysics we call this being a "critical, clinical observer," recording and reporting your dream objectively like a scientist. Suppose you were dreaming about your friend Janet. If you just wrote, "I dreamed my friend Janet and I were eating lunch" and did not describe her, it might be hard to tell if someone else had a dream with a similar element. Suppose you wrote in your journal, "My friend Janet and I were eating lunch. She is tall, skinny, has long, dark hair and is very gregarious. We were sitting at a round table in a café that looked European, with a dark interior, people laughing, and white tablecloths. I'm not sure what we were eating, but it was served in bowls." Someone else might have a dream with a person who is tall and skinny with long, dark hair, who is friendly and outgoing. They might dream of sitting at a round table with bowls of flowers. Although the other person doesn't know your friend Janet, and these are not exactly the same dreams, the elements are similar enough to be related. The accuracy and detail of reporting the dream influences how much knowledge it gives you.

In reporting dreams for the psi dreaming contests, dreamers note unexpected elements and boldface those sections of the dreams that they think or feel are particularly related to the psi content. In other words, to identify when you are receiving a telepathic message from the dream sender, or when you are dreaming a mutual dream, and to distinguish it from those dreams that are coming only from your own consciousness or purely symbolic, the self-evaluation method is to **put in bold** the dream-objects or dream-events that seem to stand out, that don't quite "fit" or belong in the dream scene or seem to be out of place.

In 2008, I participated in the dream telepathy contest at the PsiberDreaming contest. I drive long distances to teach and lecture in several different cities. The day of the contest I had spent ten hours driving in a car across four states to get to my destination. In the United States, our highways are blacktop and have yellow lines dividing the lanes. This was the dream image that kept coming to me over and over and over again: being in my car, feeling the road coming towards me, seeing the yellow lines in the road curving to the left and the woods off to the right.

I was feeling frustrated, because I really wanted to participate in this dream telepathy contest and it seemed like this day residue image was getting in the way. It kept coming at me. Several times during the night I woke up, with the same image of the road with the yellow lines curving to the left with the woods off to the right. I went ahead and submitted it. When I wrote my dream report, I put in bold face type the **road curving to the left with yellow lines.** I also wrote, the **woods off to the right**.

Understanding my own intuitive perception has been, and continues to be, a life-long process of learning to trust what I receive. This is an important key for anyone who wants to develop intuition because many people doubt themselves or second-guess themselves. I was about to do that in this case, thinking to myself that my dream image was meaningless: "Well, this is just me having been on the road all day." But I didn't. I went ahead and submitted the dream report. Learning to become intuitive means having courage, trust, willingness, and curiosity. It means being willing to put yourself on the line. As it turned out the target image that sender Dale Graff projected for this contest was Dorothy and the Tin Man and the Scarecrow on the yellow brick road. In the picture he used, the yellow road is curving to the left, with the woods to the right.

I received a fourth prize for my dream report for this contest. I learned through this process that the day residue was not clutter.

It was the way that I was receiving this image of the yellow brick road. My subconscious mind was communicating it to me with the image that was close at hand, in my brain and conscious mind, the yellow lines on the pavement with the woods off to the right.

Mutual dreaming

In the 2010 mutual dreaming contest in the PsiberDreaming Conference, Robert Waggoner volunteered to invite all of us to share his dreams. For the mutual dreaming contest, on a particular night, he was going to record his dreams. Everybody was to tune into him and then record their dreams, so the goal was for everybody to dream together, to have mutual dreams.

As I described earlier, during the PsiberDreaming Conference, there is an online message board on which people discuss the presentations they are reading and the dream experiences they are having. People comment on various discussion threads. The conference itself combines the participants' dream experiences with these online discussions.

On the night of the mutual dreaming contest I was frustrated as I had been with the telepathy contest, because all night long I kept seeing that message board from the PsiberDreaming thread over and over and over again. I saw a page with Robert Waggoner's avatar and pasQuale's avatar. Robert's avatar was like a stick figure of a guy with a hula hoop; it was pretty engaging. pasQuale, whose nickname is "Q," had an avatar that was an ornate, black "Q."

From my experience in the previous psi contests, I decided to record my dream experience even though it felt to me like pure day residue.

This is how I recorded the dream:

Title: PDC Avatars
Emotions: frustration
Structural elements: computer screen

*This was a fragment that repeated several times in the early part of the evening. I kept seeing a computer screen with **Q's avatar and Robert Waggoner's avatar.** Then I saw the block with their posts but I could not read what was written on it. I was frustrated, because in the dream I wanted to be able to read it.*

You'll see that I bolded the part that says **Q's avatar and Robert Waggoner's avatar** because that was the image that kept repeating over and over again and seemed kind of unexpected.

Then on another discussion thread, "Q" wrote this:

Post from PasQuale:

Laurel!

> **you wrote:**
> This was a fragment that repeated several times in the early part of the evening. I kept seeing a computer screen with Q's avatar and Robert Waggoner's avatar. Then I saw the block with their posts, but could not read what was written on it. I was frustrated because in the dream I wanted to be able to read it.

> **I wrote:**
> I'm writing down my first dream on the computer, when I suddenly notice that somehow I can see Robert writing something to Ed in the document I'm writing my dreams in. Robert asks something to Ed like, "Where shall I write down my dreams?" And I reply: "do it here!" and surely enough, I see Robert starting to write his dream, including sketches. He types really fast.

Then, out of the many dreams that Robert Waggoner recorded that night of the mutual dreaming contest, this was one that he titled "E-mail on the blue computer screen."

Robert Waggoner's Dream #3:

E-mail on the blue computer screen

> I see only a blue computer screen with section after section of emails (very similar to the PDC list of postings, but in an "email" type format.) I begin to scroll through them and it seems a long, long list of emails. I even see ones from myself!

pasQuale won first place in the mutual dreaming contest, and the dream image I reported received an honorable mention. This was another example of something that I thought was just day residue and, like the story I related about the dream telepathy contest, I kept trying to get this image of the computer screen out of my mind, because it kept repeating over and over.

In fact, it had a resonance with Robert Waggoner's dream and the dream that Q had.

In 2011 I had a similar experience. Robert van de Castle and Bobbie Pimm chose for the image to project a carved wooden doll with a green jacket, brown pants, orange cap and orange shirt, in a green field with mushrooms. They did a masterful job of crafting an entire day focusing on the image. At one point, Bob dressed up like the doll.

The night of the dream telepathy contest, I remembered several dreams which I reported. One of them, the first, was this one:

Dream Title: Bright Colored Clothes

Theme: Abstract colors and shapes

Emotions: Frustration and disappointment (because I wrote down the dream in more detail, thinking I was awake in physical waking reality, and then discovered I had written it down while I was still dreaming and did not remember it all upon waking up into physical waking reality.)

Major structural elements: Bright colors, clothing, abstract shapes

Intense, repeated, or unexpected elements: bright colors being thrown at me.

Dream details:

> I see a shape, oblong, rectangular, it is **translucent** and in the dream it seems like it is **absorbing something**, sort of like a sponge, but absorbing light rather than water. It has a texture kind of like rubber but not exactly, seems like a 3 or 4-dimensional piece of Scotch tape. I am aware in the dream about the telepathy contest and am thinking (in the dream) that I have to remember this to write it down.

> Then I see **clothes**, especially **shirts**, in a closet, perhaps? They are **bright colors, blue, red,** and **orange**. In the dream I am writing down the dream, thinking that it is a repeat so it must be the target. (Note: but later, when I wake up, I realize that this was a false

awakening and that there was much more to the dream that I wrote down in my dream but did not remember upon coming into physical waking reality.)

*Someone is throwing something **bright green** at me; I realize that they are **bright green shoes** and wonder if they are related to the bright colored shirts I'd seen earlier.*

The above dream is the one I believe is the reception of the telepathy target but I will submit other dream fragments also.

By this time, I remembered that the instructions for these psi contests ask dreamers to report, and put in bold face, any "intense, repeated, or unexpected elements." So this time, rather than discounting it, I paid attention to the fact that in the dream it felt like these colors were being thrown at me! Intensely, unexpectedly, and repeatedly.

When I saw the target image of the carved wooden doll with the bright colors, and when I read how often, intensely and repeatedly both Bob and Bobbie were projecting the image, I understood why it felt like the colors were being thrown at me: they were! I was receiving a mental broadcast.

Mental Broadcasting

This is how I understand what is happening in these cases. The dreamer is a Self and the mind is a vehicle for consciousness to express. The subconscious mind is where we go when we dream at night. It is where telepathy and other psi experiences occur. People are connected or related, and our subconscious minds can communicate even when we are not consciously aware of it. It is as if our minds are connected in a web. We can broadcast thoughts like a radio station broadcasts a show. When we are tuned or attentive to other people's mental broadcasts, we receive them.

The conscious mind works with the brain. It is what we are aware of when we are awake; it works with reasoning. The conscious and subconscious minds have a relationship. When the conscious mind has a desire like, "I want to receive a telepathic dream. I want to have a mutual dream. I want to remember my dreams. I want to lucid dream," it communicates that to the subconscious mind and the subconscious mind's duty is to fulfill the desire.

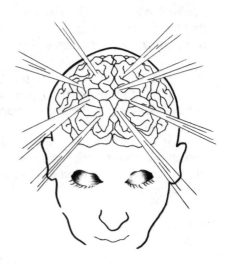

The brain is a physical organ. When we are awake, we receive information through our physical senses and store it in the brain. The more attention we give to any sense, the greater is the degree of knowledge or information we receive. The Self and the mind are not the same as the brain, but they have a relationship. The subconscious mind draws upon the information in the brain to communicate to the conscious mind, searching for the images or knowledge that most closely match what we want.

It is similar to doing an internet search. I was looking for a picture of the brain so I typed into a Google search engine "images of the brain." It came up with some 2 billion images! In the first twenty, I found one that most closely matched what I was looking for. That is similar to the way the subconscious mind draws upon what is in the brain.

The subconscious mind fulfills the conscious mind's desires and when the conscious desire is to receive telepathy or to dream together, the subconscious mind uses all that is available, including images that are in the brain that have been stored from what the thinker, or the dreamer, paid attention to during the day. So, in the telepathic dream which was my reception of Dale Graff's projection, I had the image in my brain of driving on the road all day, and that's what my subconscious mind drew upon to communicate to me the yellow brick road.

This is an example of thought projection. The recent movie *Inception* is about intentionally projecting thoughts in dreams. (See related chapter on page 179 in this book.) A lot of people were alarmed by that idea that you could actually go into someone's dream and send them a thought. I think it is comforting to know that you can communicate with people on all levels.

Mind-to-mind communication works like verbal communication. One person speaks and the other person listens. In telepathy, the sender projects the thought image. That is an aggressive or active function. It requires imagination to form an image and then to send it. Dale Graff, for example, when sending that image of the yellow brick road, dressed up like Dorothy. He acted out the image physically as well as mentally projecting the image. Bob van de Castle did the same by dressing up like the carved wooden doll, putting his hands in his pockets as the doll was, and standing in a green field with mushrooms in it.

The receiver needs to clear the mind to receive the sender's image. A clear white desk is a pretty good image for having a clear mind. The reversal exercises can be helpful for clearing your mind of conscious thinking activity so that your mind can be still to receive. When your mind is still, you can recognize a thought that is out of place or is not your thought.

Practice

I realized after the fact that in the first two dreams I mentioned, my frustration was that those images kept coming at me over and over and I couldn't get them out of my mind. This happened because I cleared my mind and asked to receive other people's images. I said, "I want to receive," so I did!

Having this happen on two occasions aided me to recognize a similar happening in last year's telepathy contest. The practice of the previous years paid off in being more cognizant of my own intuitive processes.

How do you know in a telepathic connection whose thought it is? Is it your thought, or are you receiving someone else's thought? One key is to learn when you are being aggressive, or actively thinking, and when you are being receptive or

139

expectantly waiting. If you have decided and desire to receive, be open to receiving. Clear your mind before sleep, and then trust and record anything received in the dream. If you know that upon awakening you are still-minded, the probability of having received someone else's projection is high. This is true for waking telepathy also.

It is important not to discount it or second-guess yourself. Then practice! Practice, test yourself, ask for feedback. This is why I appreciate the mutual dreaming contests and the dream telepathy contests; they are a way to learn about yourself and how your own mind works.

The metaphysical view of life is that there are Universal Laws that govern our existence. "Meta" means above or beyond, and "physics" are the physical laws of the universe. Metaphysics describes the laws of Creation, universal or mental laws. One of these is called the Universal Law of Relativity. It is very much like the internet, in which all of our minds are connected electronically. All of our minds are connected intuitively or psychically which enables this type of experience to occur.

With all of our minds connected, it seems to make sense to understand how to use this relationship for the goodness of all concerned. We can reach out to aid loved ones who are "passing on," we can pray or dream for peace. We can search for lost objects and meet our friends who live across the globe. Anything is possible.

Lucid Dreaming and Mutual Dreaming

That Recurring Dream House
... and the Door to Lucidity

I dream I am living in a house (always the same house, but not my current house) and I am walking around the house. I walk past a door and remember there is a room there that I forgot about. I go in to the room and it is a huge bedroom that looks like a theatre. Usually this part of the dreams stops here, but the last time I had it, I walked through this room and discovered three more smaller bedrooms on the other side of this room. Along with these rooms, I come upon a whole other attached apartment that I had forgotten was there. In the dream I am always feeling uneasy of the first large bedroom, but in this dream I am very excited when I discover the other three bedrooms.

This dream caught my eye when a female dreamer from the West Coast sent it in to www.dreamschool.org. It reminded me of a dream-experience I've had since childhood ... dreaming of houses with hidden passageways or secret rooms. As a child, I attributed the frequency of these dreams to my love of dollhouses and secret playhouses. As an adult student and teacher of metaphysics, I now have a different perspective on their meaning.

A couple of years ago, I started to pay attention to a recurring dream-house. I've been recording my dreams for 35 years but only recently did I note the frequency with which this particular house appears in my dreams. It intrigued me because it is not a house that is familiar in my waking state. Why was I dreaming about it? And why the same house?

As a student of metaphysics, I've learned to interpret *dream-buildings* in a universal context. Houses come in all shapes and

sizes: boxes with four walls, rounded domes, triangular-shaped tepees, igloos made of ice, buildings made of straw or corn cobs. Even with the variation of size and shape, they all serve the same function. They are dwelling places.

In the physical world, houses are places where we live. Schools are places for learning. Churches or mosques or temples are places of worship. There is a universal purpose or function of a building in our physical world.

One of my first teachers at the School of Metaphysics described an experience early in his study of metaphysics that was a key to unlocking the Universal Language of Mind. He was on a hillside, looking out over the city below. He observed all kinds of buildings: churches, schools, office buildings, and houses. Small ranch-style houses, graceful Victorian-style houses, houses made of wood, stone, and brick. He pondered who might live and use these buildings ... people of all ages, viewpoints, and backgrounds. As he gazed upon this scene, in his mind he heard the verse from the **Bible**, "In my Father's house are many mansions." (*John 14:12*)

In an intuitive flash, he realized that these buildings and houses looked distinct and the people who lived in them wore different clothes, had unique names or belonged to diverse families; yet, the houses all served the same function. They were all dwelling places. In that moment, something "clicked" and he discovered the universal nature of images or symbols. People might have a variety of thoughts or feelings or opinions about the houses in which they live, but that doesn't change the fact that the house has a universal function.

From a metaphysical perspective, we consider the "self" to be more than a physical entity, to be a soul or spiritual being. I understand dreams as experiences that come from within us, from the inner "self" or soul. Dreams reveal messages concerning this inner self or soul. The soul or inner self speaks in a universal language of pictures. So, in that light, just as a building has a universal function in the physical world, it has a corresponding function for the soul. A house in the physical world is a dwelling place; a dream-house is where the soul or inner "self" lives. The School of Metaphysics teachings call that the *mind*.

Dreams of houses or buildings tell a dreamer about his or her state of mind. The dreams are both universal and personal. For example, a church or temple universally is a place of worship in the physical world. One dreamer might view church as a place of love, comfort, and healing. Another might view church as a

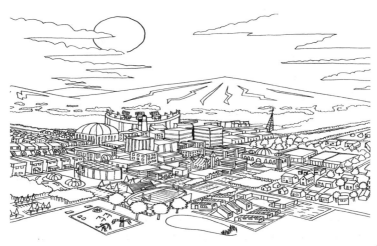

place of rules and associate it with a fear of punishment. They both have to do with a spiritual state of mind, but the dreamer's attitude about it will influence the meaning of the dream.

In the physical world, buildings have particular purposes. The way I have learned to interpret dreams, I understand that any building represents a state of mind, and the kind of building can indicate a particular kind of mind-state. So, in my dream, I'd interpret a school as a state of mind related to learning; a church or synagogue as a spiritual state of mind; a theater as a state of mind regarding the use of imagination.

You will note from the diagram on page 3 that the mind even looks like a house. The rooms on the ground floor (kitchen, living room, family room) symbolize the conscious mind, the second floor rooms or bedrooms symbolize the subconscious mind or soul, and the third floor or attic are interpreted as superconscious mind, higher self, or spirit. I understand the basement to represent that which is unconscious. Many people use a basement to store stuff they will look at "some day," junk that is not being used but which they need to examine and sort to decide what is useful and what can be thrown out. When I have dreams with a basement, I look to see what I need to become aware of and maybe "clean out" (like old attitudes that are no longer useful to me in the present).

From this perspective, when I noticed the recurring dream-house, I became interested in observing what was going on in my waking state of mind at times when I dreamed of this house. I wanted to discover what state of mind the particular dream house represented. Once I started paying closer attention to the dreams, an interesting development occurred. At first, I noticed, "I've dreamed of this house before!" only after awakening and remembering the dream. Then, *in the dream itself* I noticed that the house was familiar. I began to find new rooms in the house, ones that were added on or had previously been hidden.

There is always a feeling of exhilaration and discovery in these dreams ... curiosity about the new rooms, as if there is some secret treasure that has always been there but was previously unknown and is now about to be revealed.

Because I understand a dream-house as a symbol for a state of mind, I started to pay attention to my waking thoughts and attitudes, wondering what kind of thinking was producing this particular house in my dreams. Once I gave deeper consideration to my waking state of mind when I dreamed of this recurring house, the dream transformed even further. I'd dream of the house, notice that the house was familiar, and then, in the dream I would become aware that it was familiar because I had dreamed of it before. At this point the dream becomes lucid.

Here is an example of a progression of three dreams in a six-month period of time concerning the same dream-house:

2/09
My father and another man are looking at this house. There are rooms that go into other rooms – a hidden entrance through a closet. Another place where a door opens up to a whole other apartment. I realize that this house has been in my dreams before, and then I become lucid.

He is going through things that need to be done before it goes on the market.

6/09
The dream house/apartment I've dreamed of before. I tell S.S. and T. and their baby they can rent the apartment since there are rooms not being used by the school. Then I realize I should have asked D.S. first. Then I wonder if the money should go to the local school or to headquarters. I remember in Webster Groves it went to headquarters but I was thinking part of the idea of renting it was so the school could have some extra money since the space wasn't being used and had a separate entrance and was separated from the main school area by some space.

8/09
I am going down a steep hill. There is an apartment in a large house. At first the neighborhood seems kind of run down, but when I open the door, I see it's renovated inside and has a good feel to it. I go in one door, and realize the bigger part of the apartment next door has a separate entrance. I go in, look around, walk through

*rooms and realize there are new rooms behind one area.
It seems like every time I've gotten to the end of the
apartment there's a new section that opens up.*

*I go in and explore and notice that there are new rooms
since the last time I was there – that's when I realize I've
dreamed this house before. And then I become lucid.*

As I explored these dreams, I became aware that although I
have never seen or lived in this dream-house, it has a similar
feeling or atmosphere to the place where I first started teaching
metaphysics and directing a branch of the School of Metaphysics.
This is a different place from the one where I first became a
student of SOM. The place where I first taught and directed
was an apartment in a larger building and did, indeed, have two
entrances. Because the dream-house has a similar vibration or
feel to it as the place where I began my teaching and directing
career, this dream-house symbolizes for me the state of mind
concerning awareness of my own authority.

My father, in waking physical reality, was a teacher and
educator, as well as being my first teacher. He was also an
accomplished and charismatic public speaker. The first dream
was telling me that I was moving into a new awareness of my
own authority. I had this dream when I was learning to voice
my thoughts without being so concerned about whether other
people would agree or not. I wanted to keep my students' best
interest in mind rather than "beating around the bush" to avoid
their reaction. I was purposefully holding truth in high esteem,
when previously I had held back for fear of criticism or fear of
embarrassing someone else. The "whole other apartment" in
the dream symbolizes the new state of mind I was developing:
loving the truth and recognizing the value in voicing what I
know to be true.

In the second dream, S.S. and T. (male and female)
had a new baby, which I understand to symbolize a new idea
or new way of life. I see them both as being very expressive,
particularly emotionally, symbolizing those aspects of myself
that easily express emotion. I had that dream at a time when I
was becoming more fluent and free with using my emotions in

teaching and leading. Furthermore, I understand money in a dream to symbolize value. I was evaluating my own authority, what I personally understood and how much I was making universal principles a part of myself. (Symbolized by the concern in the dream about where the money would go.)

The third dream came when I was actively exploring (in my waking state) my ideas of leadership and teaching, becoming more clear about how to be direct and straightforward and to teach with respect. This was opening up new awarenesses in myself, reflected in the new rooms of the dream-house.

Coming down the hill could represent the challenge of being more "down to earth," and grounded rather than abstract. As a teacher, there are times that I need to give practical examples and show people through action, not just ideas, how to put into practice what I'm teaching.

Exploring New Places in Mind

When I presented this paper at the IASD PsiberDreaming Conference, one of the participants suggested that the two entrances to the house might signify my need to find another means of approach in dealing with some situation. This shed quite a bit of light for me. One of the reasons I enjoy teaching is that it stretches me to move to new places in my mind!

For example, one time I had a student with whom I was frustrated, because I didn't seem to be able to get my message across. When I spoke with my teacher about it, she said to me, "Do you think you could just love her?" Meaning that, the point (for my learning) wasn't about getting my message across or even about being heard ... it was for me to learn more about unconditional love. Another entrance! This opened my mind to an unexpected lesson or benefit from the association, not what I had originally anticipated.

In waking physical reality, the building where I started teaching metaphysics was in Ann Arbor, Michigan, an apartment above a storefront. It had one entrance and two stories. There was an attached apartment next door. At one point, the landlord changed the way he rented the space, so that instead of two stories, we had one floor side-by-side. The door to the side apartment (that had previously been locked) was then opened so that we could have the two adjacent spaces. The door to the upstairs that had previously been opened, was then locked.

So, the similarity in the dream-house to the waking house was the apartment with two entrances, with one entrance that had previously been unused later opening up to reveal a new, useable space. I have discovered that I dream of this place when something like this is occurring in my consciousness; for example, "unlocking" my ability to love more unconditionally and to become more accepting.

These discoveries about my own recurring dream-house were exciting, and I asked other people if they ever had a house that recurred in their dreams. I received an overwhelming "yes" response. The progression I discovered from my own dreams was replicated by many others:

1. Becoming aware upon awakening that there is a house that the dreamer has dreamed of before.
2. Having dreams in which the dream-house appears, and the dreamer is aware *in the dream* that it is a familiar house, often with new rooms or improvements that have been made in the house.
3. Dreaming of the house, becoming aware in the dream that the house is familiar and often it is changed or improved, then becoming aware that it is familiar because the dreamer has dreamed of it previously ... an "aha!" moment ... and then the dreamer becomes lucid.

This is particularly intriguing to me because I have not been a frequent lucid dreamer. I've learned that this dream-house is a "doorway" into lucid dreams for me. Since making this discovery, I've also discovered a dream-dormitory that appears in my dreams. Although I did live in a dormitory for my first year of college as a freshman, and again when I transferred to a new school as a junior for my first year there, the dream-dormitory is not one I ever lived in, nor is it one I ever saw.

Security and Value

Reviewing my journals over time, I have noticed an interesting pattern in the dormitory dreams. In many of them, I am wandering the halls, trying to find my room, and there is some concern about losing my purse, or being afraid that someone has stolen my money.

Following are three examples of this kind of dream:

I am at some college, in the dormitory with a couple of my friends. We're walking the halls and I realize that I forgot something in my room. Then I realize I've been here before and I feel uneasy. When I get to the room, I am panicked when I discover that my roommate has left the keys in the door and the door is slightly open, not locked. I open the door, afraid that my money is gone and am relieved to find that my purse is where I left it.

Another dream:
I am trying to find my room in the dorm. There are circular halls and I think I have found the right one, but then find that the staircase doesn't go to the floor I thought it would. It seems like I should know where to go so I am getting afraid. Suddenly, I realize that I don't have my wallet with me and get frantic, trying to remember where I left it. I go back to the lounge area and I find it hidden behind a couch cushion and figure it fell out of my pocket and I hadn't noticed.

A third one:
I am in a college dorm, wandering around the halls. It seems familiar but I can't seem to find where I am supposed to go. I leave my purse and notebook on a couch where MB and a guy are horsing around.

When I wander I am going up and down staircases and in different rooms. When I come back, my purse is gone. I am very upset. There was a lot of cash in my wallet. I curse, like I can't believe it happened. MB is in the room and she seems oblivious.

> *A black girl I don't know pulls a purse from behind a couch. She says, "Is this it?" It is. I look through it and the money is all there. There's a $100 bill, two $50 bills and some other money. I am very grateful.*
>
> *The girl says, "Next time, call." I say, "That's why I came back — it felt like it was getting late." She asks who was watching it. I don't want to embarrass MB so I just say, "someone who is in this room." She still doesn't even acknowledge that she was supposed to be watching my purse." (I am irritated at her.)*

When I first recorded these dreams I did not pay attention to the fact that the dormitory dreams also had the common theme of being afraid of losing my wallet or purse. Only upon reviewing my dream journals did I notice that all of the dreams with the recurring dream dormitory have a theme of losing, or being afraid of losing, my purse or wallet, or finding the door unlocked, or being worried that I left the door unlocked.

In other words, they all have to do with questions of security or lack thereof. This was a great revelation to me, because although I knew that the dream-dormitory recurred with a similar pattern as the dream-house, it was only upon reflection that I saw the relationship of the dormitory dreams and the security theme. This gave me insight — the dream dormitory occurs when, in my waking state, I am feeling insecure about something that I am learning.

Contemplating these dreams, I now see that they relate to times in my life when I am learning something that is not brand new but more like a further development of things I have already understood to some extent. (I see this symbolized by the college setting, since college is an institution of higher learning.) When I have been insecure (the keys in the lock, door left open) or think that I should already know something that I have not yet mastered, it appears in the dream as fear of being lost, or losing my purse or wallet. The money symbolizes value, and the fear in these dreams that my money is gone relates to my own doubts (when awake) about my value. Do I know enough? Shouldn't I already know this? These concerns are reflected in these dreams.

Further reflection helped me to see that my attitude that "I should already know this" is not really honest. The dormitory is a place to live while in college, and one has to go through primary and secondary education to be able to go to college. So I assumed, at first, that this dream-setting symbolized a state of mind in which I should be more advanced than I felt I was. Yet, in my physical waking experience, I only lived in a dormitory when I was at a new school for the first time. So in truth these dreams reflect a state of mind in which I need to admit my inexperience. I am the most insecure when I am taking a new step to go beyond what I already know, in the first stages of a new development in myself.

The dreams are showing me that I need to give myself credit for what I already have, or to recognize that I have more value than I think I do. I see this in the repeated theme of being afraid that I have lost my money or that it has been stolen, and then, in the end, finding (with relief!) the purse or discovering that the money is safe after all.

It is highlighted in the last dream by the friend, MB, who I was expecting to watch my purse. She symbolizes to me an aspect of myself that is often riddled with doubt. She is a wonderful person but has challenges with self value, so it made sense that she was the dream-character in this scene, and that I was irritated with her. In my waking state, I get irritated with myself when I am insecure!

Seeing patterns like this is one benefit I have discovered from looking at dreams over time. One at a time, I had not noticed that the dreams in the dormitory all had some theme of losing money. The recurrence of this related theme helped me to make sense of my own attitudes when I am learning something new and think I should already know it, or when I am taking for granted my own understanding and value, fearing that I don't know enough. Once I observed this, I made changes in my waking life, becoming more gentle and compassionate with myself when learning something new.

This valuable insight has helped me to be a better student of life and self awareness ... I haven't had any of the dormitory dreams since this evaluation!

Healing and House Dreams

As I shared my experiences with the recurring dream house, other people reported houses that repeated in their dreams as well. Many discovered that as they were becoming aware of old ways of thinking or healing past trauma, their dreams reflected this. One dreamer said:

> I too am fascinated by house dreams and have them all the time. It makes sense that recognition of a dream house from waking life would create the perfect doorway to lucid dreaming. It reminds me of a series of nightmares I had in my tumultuous 20s where I would wake up IN the dream from a dream of someone or something chasing me and turn on the light by the bed and the light would not turn on, thus intensifying my terror tenfold. In some of the dreams, I would go so far as to get up and turn on the wall light switch and it too would not turn on the lights, hence more terror, then I would actually wake up and frantically turn on the light. This series lasted many years and occurred at multiple locations. Obviously, I was seeking the light of source in a dark and confusing time in my life. I can see now that if I'd more knowledge of lucid dreaming and tools to work with how it might have been an easy step to go lucid.
>
> Since I began to actively study dreams in the past year and grown leaps and bounds as a result of new found inner resources and awareness, my house dreams have often been dreams with new and expansive hidden rooms or even gardens, new apartments I'm moving into (with various people), places I used to live but am now leaving, as well as new construction dreams. I often recognize dream houses as places I have been before in my dreams.

Knowing that a house symbolizes the mind may influence the dream itself, contributing to a dreamer's lucidity. This appears in the following dream of a School of Metaphysics student who is actively involved in healing some old attitudes. She dreams of a recurring house. She became lucid (as I have) when she recognized the familiar house in her dream. Here is her dream and interpretation of it:

The Haunting
I dreamed of going into a house that I have dreamed about before. I am there with my sister C. I look at the inside. It is empty. It is also very large.

I look at the kitchen that turns into a great room-living room area. There are several bedrooms on the right side of the room. As I continue to walk through the house I see that there is more space and rooms than I thought there were. There is a perfect space for an office. As I continue I realize that there are more rooms on the other side of the wall, a whole living quarters with kitchen and bedrooms. It was like a duplex but all connected. I realize as I am looking at this place and that I want to buy it. I see so much space, there is no furniture at this time.

I look through the place again thinking how nice and spacious it is then I start to recognize the second side of the house. At this point I become lucid. I realize that I have dreamed about this house before and it has always had a leaking ceiling with water actively running into the room and peeling paint. Now the house is in good repair and beautiful. I wonder why I am here.

Then I realize one of the bedrooms in the house is haunted and want to know why this is occurring. I go to look at the room. It had a large TV in the room easily seen from the doorway. I am standing on the side of the door wondering what would happen next. As C... sits down in a chair opposite the door to the room the ghost, which looks like a ball of energy, comes out of the TV and fires energy at her.

I realize that the ghost represents the misuse of my imagination that occurred during the previous day. Then I wake up.

The dreamer said, "This dream relates to an experience I had during the previous day where I had let my imagination get the better of me. I was reacting to losing some papers at the school where I teach. I was feeling very responsible for the loss and felt I was to blame. I was imagining everyone's displeasure of me and thought they found me lacking in my responsibility. I was feeling like a failure in general.

The dream highlighted to me that I wasn't a failure. I had made changes in my thinking, symbolized by the house in good repair. I needed to stay open to learning, realizing that I had a lot of attachment to looking good and being perfect, the haunting. This dream helped me to relax and find the objectivity I needed so I could stay open to learning."

This dreamer contributed her dream to the School of Metaphysics www.dreamschool.org website. Dr. Barbara O'Guinn Condron, the International Education Coordinator and director of this dream education site, commented on K's dream: "This is an evolved way of understanding how health appears in a dream. Most people do not realize how what we imagine is the source of most of the fears we will ever experience.

Particularly noteworthy in your description is the moment of lucidity. There is a clear demarcation between the known, older side of the house which reminds me of Jesus' quote that 'in my father's house are many mansions.' Your house includes a section under renovation, which is a wonderful representation of healing. It also includes the haunted room which indicates that what is persecuting you is contained in one space, one group of attitudes, and they are all linked to whatever your sister represents and other people's thoughts.

Whether this is the reason for the 'haunting' or its remedy, only you can say."

Moving Out ... Into a New Way of Life

In waking physical reality, people move into a new home when they are making a change. Adolescents leave their parents' home to go to college, or move out to gain independence. Often married couples buy a house as their first joint venture. Some retirees move from an older family home to something smaller and more conducive to their new lifestyle.

Just as a physical move represents a change in consciousness, some people move out of a dream house when they are changing old attitudes and moving to new ones.

For example, a dreamer who is a psychoanalyst noticed a correlation between healing emotional issues and a change in his recurring house dreams:

> *For 15 years of therapy, I dreamed of being back in my childhood home. In one of my first lucid dreams I finally packed my stuff and left, flying away. I was leaving my childhood home [in my dreams] when I had worked through the issues that had me stuck there.*

Another dreamer recognized that the recurring home from childhood appeared in her dreams as a symbol of the depressed state of mind she experienced while awake. As she received counseling, moving beyond anti-depressant medication to a more lucid waking state, she noticed a change in the dreams. She moved out of the old dilapidated house as she moved out of depression into peace of mind:

> *Moving out*
> *Another house dream that I have is a home from childhood. When I was younger we moved to a home that was practically falling down. It had holes in the floor. It was really awful. The dream is a nightmare and based on this house.*
>
> *I am back in West Liberty and the house is in worse condition than when I was a kid. It is falling down around me, but I am trying to fix the roof and the walls. By the end of the dream I am able to get the roof to stop caving in and the walls in some parts of the house are straight again.*

157

This dream is such a nightmare for me. I really hated living there and would not even want to live in the town let alone the house. This dream has to get really bad for me to be lucid. In fact, I am usually quite frustrated with the repairs and realize I will go bankrupt trying to fix the house. It is at this point I realize 1. I hate the house and, 2. I am dreaming. It is at this point I am calm again because I realize I can walk away. And I do, to the next dream.

Lucid When Awake ... Lucid Dreaming

The same dreamer noticed a pattern in her dreams of houses. She has another dream-house, one that is enjoyable with secret passageways. The more conscious she is, when awake, of her attitudes, and the more consciously she pursues knowledge of her own mind, the less frequently she dreams of this house. It is as if she "moves in" to the dream house when she needs to pay attention to her own mind:

The most common house dream for me is a very large house with many levels and rooms (the levels have increased over the years. It started with two and has grown to four). I have had this dream since childhood and it stopped while I was a student at the School of Metaphysics. It has recently came back. [since discontinuing my studies at the SOM.] I know the house well and I realize in the dream that it is from a long time ago (by this I mean another life; although I believe this realization is part of the dream). This is when I am aware that I am dreaming and am happy to be back. I can explore many rooms, however right now I really do not recall any room except the kitchen. This is the most common part of the dream. There is a back staircase to the kitchen and I believe it is a secret that only I know about. I love to use this entrance and am often playing with other children when I decide to go to the kitchen. (I am usually a child in the dream, however when I realize it is a dream I am an adult. It is like an instant change.)

Since the dream has started again I am more often an adult with kids and the kitchen has more expensive items. In fact the staircase has expensive items along it. They are Egyptian and I recognize they are very valuable. I am upset because I lived in the house when I was a child and the house is no longer mine. I want the house and the items again because they are valuable. But, I am torn because I believe the items should be returned to the rightful owners.

The dreamer understands this house represents her desire to "come as little children" as it says in the **Bible**, to be open and receptive to new learning about herself. I understand the kitchen to symbolize a place for acquiring knowledge. You might consider food in a dream to be a symbol for knowledge, as reflected in our saying, "food for thought." This dreamer believes that when she was consciously pursuing the development of her mind as a student of metaphysics, she stopped having the dream because the self-knowledge was no longer secret. When she became more involved with her career and motherhood and less involved with her own spiritual development, the exploration of her mind happened at night ... in this dream house!

You will note that in the dream she longs for ownership of the house and its valuable contents, showing her that knowing herself and her own mind is very important to her sense of well-being.

House as Metaphor

When I presented this study of recurring house dreams at the IASD PsiberDreaming Conference, Massimo Schinco, a psychotherapist from Italy, made an astute connection between house dreams and patients with dementia. He recognized that these patients' waking thoughts might be related to the symbolism of a house representing the mind.

"The house as a symbol of mind suggests to me a connection with ... people suffering Alzheimer and dementia. Very often people in dementia have the compulsion to 'go back home' (even when they are already at home!). Perhaps they are searching for having their mind back, the mind that they have lost because of their disease."

This observation made sense to me, as people with dementia exist in a kind of in-between state, sometimes existing in subconscious reality (where dreams occur) and confusing it with physical reality. On a related note, many people associated the feeling of "being at home" with another person as being at ease with that person, having a soul-to-soul or mind-to-mind connection.

Taking Care of Your Dream House

I believe that the more each one of us knows our own mind, the more effectively we live our lives. We can be happy, healthy, and holy (whole). If you have houses in your dreams, you might begin to notice if the same house recurs. Then, here are some suggestions for how you might use these dreams for greater lucidity:

- Pay attention to the recurring dream house
- Note any features that stay the same
- Note any features that change
- Identify what is occurring in your waking attitudes when you dream of this house
- Identify what is changing in your waking attitudes when there are new rooms or renovations in the house
- Note if it is a house familiar to you in waking physical reality or if it has similar characteristics to some house you've known in waking physical reality

I understand houses or buildings in general to symbolize a state of mind, so the key (I've found) to understand the house-in-the-dream is to become aware of the waking state of mind that precipitates it.

The more AWAKE I've become, or the more aware I've become about my waking attitudes, then the more likely it is for the dream to become lucid.

If you have a recurring dream-house, whether it's the house you live in or a house that only appears in your dreams, my recommendation is to pay attention to your waking state of mind. See if there are any correlations or similarities to what's occurring in your waking state when you have the house dreams.

I expect that as you become more aware of your state of mind in waking physical reality, you will find new rooms in your dream-house, indicating you are discovering something new in yourself.

Inception:
Who's Controlling Your Mind?

The 2010 movie *Inception* stirred a lot of people. Few movies have generated such publicity in major media. The *Today Show, Good Morning America*, even the *Wall Street Journal*, featured news stories about the film. Why was it so controversial? What stimulated everyone's curiosity ... or fear?

The film is a fictional account of a character named Dom Cobb who is a thief, hired to steal or "extract" corporate secrets from the subconscious mind of business owners while they sleep. In this plot, Cobb is hired for an even greater task: "incepting" or planting an idea in the subject's dreaming mind. Is this possible? Can one enter another person's dreams?

The film raises questions about the mind, questions which few people can answer. Can people dream together? Is one's mind vulnerable to being penetrated by another mind, especially a mind with evil intent?

Part of the intrigue of this film is the blending of truth and fiction. Many people have experienced a "false awakening" in a dream; that is, thinking that they have awakened, only to find out that they are still dreaming. This surreal experience is depicted in the film. Many people feel a "jerk" or a "kick" when becoming aware of going into a deeper state of sleep, or coming up into a more shallow one. This dream experience is shown in the film as well.

But what about the rest of it? Do people need to fear being invaded while asleep? Upon first viewing *Inception* I was disappointed at the violence in it. The dream space and experience, for many of us who pay attention to dreams, was too harsh. It seemed more Hollywood-ish than dreamlike. My dreams, even nightmares, are ethereal, not so loud. Yet, there were enough dreamy scenarios to raise questions about what happens during that inner experience we call dreaming.

Perhaps director Christopher Nolan has dreams like the scenes in the film. He told ABC News reporters that the inspiration for the film came from his own lucid dreaming experiences. "I wanted to do this for a very long time; it's something I've thought about off and on since I was about 16," Nolan told *The Los Angeles Times* last year. "I wrote the first draft of this script seven or eight years ago, but it goes back much further, this idea of approaching dream and the dream life as another state of reality."[1]

When I heard so many people were talking about the movie I decided it was worth watching again. This time I went with a notebook and pen, and took notes. I've never done that before, but there was so much dialogue loaded with information, I wanted to make sure to capture the ideas presented and not just the emotional and sensual barrage.

This proved to be fruitful. I came away from the second time watching the movie with much deeper thoughts about its meaning and how people might use it.

In my view, this movie is more about thought form projection than about dreams. The dream is the place, the scene. The subject matter, the plot itself, seemed to be about mind control. Who controls whose mind? What happens when our own thoughts and emotions are out of control? Is it possible to manipulate someone else's mind or is it only our own unconscious stuff that manipulates us?

One of the principles of thought projection, or what some people call "mind control" is that yours is the mind to control. Think about it ... if your own mind is full of fear, how effective can you be communicating with someone else? If you hold a grudge against another person or harbor guilt and resentment, does it not color how you relate to that person?

Resolving unfinished business is an essential element in peace of mind. People who have a hard time living life, or who fear death, often have such issues to resolve. Clearing your own mind of hidden guilt, disappointment, or regret gives you understanding and, therefore, control of your own life. Ultimately this seems to me to be one lesson that can be learned from the film.

Inception is a complex portrayal of what happens when a group decides to dream together. It is definitely a movie, and many of its plot lines and visuals seem to be pure entertainment (for those who are entertained by explosions and gunfire!). At the same time, I was intrigued to see the writers depict some truths about the mind.

Some of the details were interesting, such as the "kick" to indicate the jolt of falling awake, a relatively common occurrence. Also familiar is incorporating sensations in physical waking reality into the dream, like the water in the bathtub producing a flood in the dream or hearing music in the dream that is playing in the physical world. Many of us have experienced this in the dreamtime.

More intriguing to me was the story about how one person can suggest a thought in a way that another person will receive it. Dom, the main character who has experience with "inception", teaches us the principles:

The seed thought has to be fully formed for it to "take" in the mind of the receiver. Once one receives it, he or she can't get it out, and it grows, both while the person is dreaming and once awake. It has to harmonize with his own thinking; in other words, the receiver needs to be inspired. It must seem to him that he originated the idea or else it will seem like a foreign idea and he'll resist or get defensive. *Inception* shows this when, in the dream world, his "projections" (dream-people) start to stare and then become hostile because they know that something or someone is intruding.

I've heard people discuss their fears after seeing this movie. They are afraid that someone might be able to plant an idea in their mind. But, don't we experience that every day, with advertising? Don't many people listen to music with lyrics that "they can't get out of their head"? The key to alleviating the fear in all of this comes when Cobb counsels the dream inceptors to choose a positive thought form. The idea has to strike the dreamer's emotions, and, he says, "Positive emotion always trumps negative."

> *What if we chose to dream together to live according to common values?*

In other words, the mind to control is your own. When you know who you are, when you are clear about your ideals and your core values, you will know if a negative idea, one that is not yours, is being projected to you. When you strengthen your will by making choices to live according to your ideals, you don't have to worry about being pulled astray. You can accept anything that harmonizes with your values and reject what doesn't.

We do this every day. We are barraged with ideas, information, products, sounds, smells, and sights. We do not eat every bit of food that is offered to us. We don't buy every available product. When we know what we believe, and what we value, we can discern right from wrong, good from evil, and wholesome from unhealthy. We do not have to be subject to other people's ill intent, even if it exists (as it does in this movie). We can choose to create positive, uplifting, light-filled thoughts.

Perhaps it doesn't make for great entertainment, but think of the potential for humanity if we could harness this ability to implant positive and desirable thought forms that are stronger and more resilient than negative ones. Thoughts like living in a peaceful world, everyone on the planet practicing the Golden Rule, harmonizing with nature. What if we chose to dream together to live according to common values? Is this a waking dream or something we can dream into waking, physical reality?

Upon seeing the film a second time, I am of the opinion that the movie's primary theme is reality. What is reality? Is waking physical reality the true reality or is the dream world the true reality? What happens when we have unresolved emotional business? It becomes our reality ... breaking into our dreams, our present relationships, and our state of mind whether awake or asleep. It interferes with our own and other people's existence.

Learning how to understand and learn from our dreams can aid us to understand our waking reality, and vice versa. In which world are we the most awake?

These are questions that stimulate people to explore the dream world. At one point, the dream architect Ariadne describes forming the landscape of the dream world as "pure creation." Once she has a taste, she can't stay away from it. Cobb and his wife Mal got addicted to the "high" of pure creation, and became lost there. Is this possible? Can we really get lost in this world of the subconscious?

Yes, we can ... but we don't have to. Just as the Ariadne of mythology led Theseus to the opening of the maze once he had defeated the Minotaur, so *Inception*'s Ariadne helps Dom Cobb face and defeat the monsters in his unconscious, so that he can open the door to embrace waking physical reality. He can be more lucid when awake because he has become more lucid in his dreams!

Myth? Entertainment? Yes, and also one of the ways that our dreams can aid us to live in light.

The College of Metaphysics is a center for intuitive research, including the practical application of psi dreaming. When faced with the opportunity for a choir to practice an upcoming cantata in their nighttime dreams, Dr. Barbara O'Guinn Condron, a prioneer in the field of Group Dreaming, developed a Global Lucid Dreaming Experiment (GLiDE) to observe and record the results. I asked Dr. O'Guinn Condron to contribute this chapter to show how group dreaming can unite people inwardly, even when their physical bodies are in 8 different cities. This experiment in group dreaming sheds light on the power of the mind and its potential to bring people together across time and distance for group creation, cooperation, and harmony.

The Dream
Consciousness
Circuit
When Choirs Dream Together

Barbara O'Guinn Condron D.M., D.D.

A couple years ago, I had the pleasure of meeting Viki Andersen. Viki is the producer of a film series called *Dreamtime* that aired on PBS. Her research introduced her to dozens of dreamers, professionals and laypeople, and gave her a global education in dreaming.

When it came down to the essence of humanity dreaming, Viki experienced a startling revelation. "What fascinated me was the idea that throughout time, in all cultures, someone has always been dreaming," she said, her eyes lighting up. "No matter what the time, someone has *always* been dreaming, as far back as we can imagine!"

Viki's observation echoed in my mind as I surveyed the data we collected from the 24 people in our cantata group. They remembered a total of 720 dreams, with one woman remembering dreams 78 of the 80 nights the study covered.

Reading the dream records, I thought to myself, "Someone was always dreaming." The dream records our choir members kept became one of the largest and most precise documentations of group dreaming ever assembled. How this came to be, what it says about humanity's capacity for interaction in the dream state, and the implications for you, your family, and even those you have yet to meet will surprise, delight, and inspire you. Here is the multidimensional story. Katrina is a member of our musical ensemble. Here is her dream journal entry from late October, midway into our rehearsals for a holiday time presentation.

Dream Journal: Katrina, female 10.24.10

*I was in the upper level of the Peace Dome. We were
sitting around the outside perimeter in a large circle. Dr.
Barbara Condron* [the cantata's director] *was leading
a discussion about the cantata. A lady I serve at work
said, "I think we should get a cheese truck, and take it to
all the cheese festivals, to dance at the cheese festivals."*

Matt [choir director] *says, "I want a radio truck so we
can travel around and do radio."*

Dr. Laurel Clark [SOM President] *is sitting next to Dr.
Barbara and she says, "Matt, if you want to do radio I
will teach you."*

*We got up and walked out of the Peace Dome and
into my parent's house. Dr. Terry Martin* [teacher] *said
she wants to get the music down enough to be able to
sing "Kyrie". I told her that I know the song because
I learned it in high school. She told me that she knew
that and I had such good training from Mr. Palmeri*
[teacher]. *I think that I should find Palmeri and let him
know about my performance.*

The dreamer is a 30-year-old chef born in Poughkeepsie, New York. For two months, she has been taking a class in performing arts at the College of Metaphysics (COM) in Missouri. She portrays Elizabeth, sister of Mary and mother of John (the Baptist) in a musical presentation called *The Christ Seed*. The play was presented in the Peace Dome[1] in December 2010.

All the characters in her dream are people she knows. Five of them are involved in music, both in the woman's present and her past. Three hold doctorates in metaphysics. Three are involved in the performance.

Is Katrina's dream reflecting her life or is her life reflecting her dream? One month later, on November 21 she writes, "*I was rehearsing the Cantata in my dreams all night long. Running through the whole thing from beginning to end over and over, refining it."* Each month, she shows measurable improvement in her characterization, her singing and her movement.

If Katrina is dreaming of the cantata, what are the other 21 singers dreaming? Is singing and rehearsing present in their dreams? Do they dream about one another? Faculty and students at the School of Metaphysics[2] (SOM) have been answering questions like these for years.

What happens when someone begins recording, studying, and interpreting their own dreams? Students have been answering *that* question since 1973.

What happens when those students of Mind compose music for words from the **Bible** and the **Tao Te Ching**, or from the prayers of indigenous people? This is a question teachers at SOM have been answering since 1983.

What happens when teachers who are awake in their dreams come together to dream during the day? SOM researchers at the College of Metaphysics have been answering this question with the Global Lucid Dreaming Experiments since 2007.

The world of daytime artistic dreaming and night-time scientific dreaming came together in such a natural way. These questions and their answers merged in the fall of 2010 when two dozen people, all SOM students who record their dreams, started meeting at the world's Peace Dome to do something together that they all love — singing!

> *We are the music makers and we are the dreamers of dreams.*[3]
> *–Arthur O'Shaughnessy, British poet*

Located on the campus of the College of Metaphysics, the Peace Dome is a three-story monolithic dome rising from the countryside in south central Missouri. It was dedicated as a universal site for peace in 2003. Since then, students at the college come together to offer a holiday program interweaving songs of the season with the *Universal Peace Covenant*[4], a 577-word document created in 1996-97. The dome creates what is called a whispering gallery with acoustical properties such that a faint sound may be heard around its entire circumference. Singing in the dome is a rare delight.

In 2010, the program evolves. Auditions are open to anyone currently studying at the School of Metaphysics (SOM). Twenty-three singers from seven states are selected.

Participants meet once a month for four weekends to  rehearse the elements of the performance. The remainder of the month, the seventeen women and six men live their chosen lives as a homeopathic doctor, electronics engineer, yoga instructor, chef, human resources administration, nurse, biofeedback specialist, attorney, landlord, web designer, teacher, student, minister, or writer in cities like Chicago, Dallas, and Louisville. The varied group ranges in age from 15 to 64, from high school student to post-college grad. Most identify themselves as Christian or Interfaith, and a few have no affiliation or consider themselves "spiritual."

Because they are students enrolled at SOM, they are invested in mind and consciousness development, practicing daily mental exercises in concentration, meditation, and visualization. Logging mind experiences, particularly dreams, is a class requirement.

One of the first practical concepts SOM students learn is the difference between an ideal and a goal. A goal describes what you want — oatmeal with raisins is a goal when you are hungry. An ideal related to that goal might be wholesome, nutritious food grown organically by people with an expanded consciousness of global connection. Ideals include others. They move out of personal space thinking and enter into the larger realm of interpersonal space. That's why ideals require mind investment. Because I am expecting my students to think with their minds, the instructions I give need to encourage that engagement.

When the mind rests upon an ideal, it considers the highest good the thinker is capable of imaging. Ideals exercise the imagination. Imagination says, "*What if* everyone in the world had food to eat?" The 15-year-old in the cantata choir reflects the interpersonal ideal: "to contribute to the creation of this incredible musical experience and help spread the joy of it across the land."[5] One woman states her ideal simply as "Rhythm and Joy,"[6] both being personal and interpersonal. Another woman describes a personal ideal, "As a lifelong student of scripture and a teacher of it in my past, I continue to search out the Truth it has for us... My ideal is to grow more into Christ consciousness by greater understanding of the qualities of thought that it embodies."[7]

Once the ideal is set, the mind is pressed into service to create purpose for personal involvement. Purpose, then, is the individual's function within the ideal. Purpose defines the role that person will play and how will it transform him or her. The purposes are varied: "*to expand my understanding of the quality of love as a creative force and to understand the open heart,*"[8] "*to experience consciously in order to know the science and workings of the mind,*"[9] and "*to develop a deeper understanding of the productive use of music to aid myself and others to inspire, to motivate, and to heal.*"[10]

One student reflects what I presented as the ideal and purpose of the cantata itself when she describes her ideal is "*Meditative Consciousness. The singing, breathing, connection, holy works, and attuning to greater energies will aid in this.*" The *Christ Seed* is the second of a three-part musical arc that began with a production called *The Power of Prayer around the World* and will culminate with *The Revelation of God in Man.* This cantata is meant to cultivate meditative consciousness in the performers. The student's purpose is "*to uplift my consciousness and develop devotion and gratitude.*"[11] As this is manifested in the individual performers, the entire presentation will manifest its purpose as well.

The Christ Seed is meant to stimulate the idea within the audience of Christlike thought. We want the audience to experience a notable internal shift in consciousness from the moment they enter the Peace Dome to the moment they leave.

To accomplish this in one hour will require significant depths of understanding in the collective mind *of the choir*. When present, this depth will translate into what choir members do with their voices, instruments, and movement.

We are creating consciousness in motion, arising from harmonious individual contributions. This begins with an ideal, and I must determine the point origin for the students. Toward this end, I give them a question to answer: *When and how I became aware of the Christ seed in me?*

Their responses are remarkable, reflecting the consciousness that reaches beyond physical prejudice, expanding consciousness into the possibilities of connection possible in nonphysical realities. I will share two responses from two very different people. First, Golbahar. Why is a young woman, born in Iran and raised in a Muslim family, participating in a musical presentation telling the story of the birth of Jesus? For the physically-minded, the prospect is hardly conceivable. For someone desiring to experience a greater Truth, it makes all the sense in the world.

Part of Golbahar's motivation for being in this class is to learn more about the **Bible** and how it can be interpreted in the same language as the language in dreams. She writes:

"When I was 12 years old, I remembered sitting in the schoolbus in Iran, going around the city as the children got dropped off. There was a particular street that we would pass

by every day and it was a less fortunate part of the city. There, I remember having the question come to me, 'Are there evil people in the world?' It was such a burning question, deep inside of me, I thought I would burst if I did not have an answer! I thought about it for a long time and I couldn't convince myself that any human could be inherently evil or bad or wrong? I decided to take a survey. So, I asked everyone I knew, and everyone had the same answer. 'Well, of course, there are evil people in the world!' Then they would proceed to give me examples. I never could believe them. It felt like that could not be true. It never resonated. I came to the conclusion that all people have good in them. I didn't have the proof, so I was not yet a knower, but I believed.

"Now that years have passed, I see what it is about. It was me at a young age recognizing that all humans have the Christ Seed within. I had an understanding of this, and the question was the stimulus that became a life-long quest to find the answer. The reason it was hard for me to think otherwise is because I recognized the Christ Seed within myself. I knew there was more to me than what meets the naked eye and so I concluded that there was more to everyone. It is this question that led me to a self-awareness training in 2007 and exactly a year later to the School of Metaphysics. So that I could uncover that 'more' that I knew is inside."[12]

At the other end of the spectrum is Ryan, the self-described "Christian(ish)" electronics engineer, who will portray Jesus. This is how he describes his journey to *The Christ Seed*.

"The first time I embraced the Christ Seed as Present Moment Knowing was preparing for a talk that I was to give at a church retreat with my high school youth group. I reviewed my favorite book at the time, The Screwtape Letters by C. S. Lewis and was struck by the chapter about time. He explained that the chief problem for humanity is our distraction with the past and the future and further stated that humans can only connect with our immortal, spiritual nature in the one moment in time that is touched by the divine light of eternity, the present moment.

"This awakened in me an inner knowing that the "Kingdom of God is at hand" and it became the central focus for my talk. It was also the first inkling I received that salvation was far more than some mysterious phenomenon that affected my afterlife only. That same weekend I was given a book called A New Kind of Christian by Brian McClaren which helped me to see that there is *the possibility for profound spiritual practice outside the context of rigid doctrine. It would still be a few years of college before I really took on the mantle of personal responsibility regarding my relationship with mystery, but this is where my mind began to open to possibilities.*

"It was actually a Buddhist author, Sogyal Rinpoche, who introduced me to the benefits of regular disciplined practice that inspired me to find the School of Metaphysics and it was at the School of Metaphysics that my Christ Seed was for the first time and continues to be directly and purposefully nurtured."[13]

When called upon to write *ideal* and *purpose* papers, students direct their attention inward, exploring and developing their own ideas, molding them until the appropriate words are chosen to reflect those thoughts. This forges a strong base for the inner work that will be reflected in their day and night-time dreams. Reading these papers in class begins the creative process by establishing the group consciousness upon which the outer work of performance depends. As you will see, their visualization work affects the performance, both awake and asleep.

Early on, I realize we have a unique opportunity to study the dreams of people who are pursuing a common goal. Since 2007, researchers at the College of Metaphysics have studied data collected by 961 dreamers from 21 countries on seven different topics ranging from the moon's effect on dreaming to solutions for economic challenges in our lives. In those Global Lucid Dreaming Experiments[14], SOM students form a unique control group. Since this particular study is driven not by a dream hypothesis, rather a common creative goal, we are open to whatever the dreams reveal.

Do people who sing together, dream together? This seemed like the perfect time to find out.

The Dream Consciousness Circuit

Now that the personal ideals and purposes are moving in the participants' minds, it is time to direct this powerful creative force toward common ideals. These arise from the songs within the cantata, the words and music they will be bringing to life. Communication — particularly telepathy — will be a mainstay of our performance. Mind maps are the tool we use to engage whole brain involvement and to strengthen communication between the Conscious Mind and the Subconscious Mind. Words reflect Conscious thinking, and pictures or images communicate Subconscious thinking. When both are present, something I call the Dream Consciousness Circuit[15] is connected.

THE DREAM CONSCIOUSNESS CIRCUIT

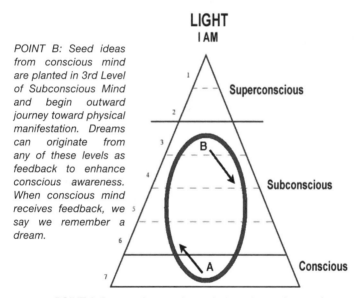

POINT B: Seed ideas from conscious mind are planted in 3rd Level of Subconscious Mind and begin outward journey toward physical manifestation. Dreams can originate from any of these levels as feedback to enhance conscious awareness. When conscious mind receives feedback, we say we remember a dream.

POINT A: Dreamer's conscious mind receives a dream. Once interpreted and applied to the waking life, a new desire arises from the conscious mind to be fulfilled by the subconscious mind, either as a manifestation of that desire in the waking life, or as feedback from subconscious mind in the form of a dream.

Creating mind maps of the conceptual meaning of the music is a way of illustrating the student's own understanding of the message s/he wants to convey. Diagrams comprised of symbols — words, pictographs, and images — have been used for centuries to organize, illustrate, and describe idea relationships. An excellent book on the topic is *The Mind Map Book*[16] by Tony Buzan.

After auditions during the first month, the class was divided into two groups. Most became the "choir of angels," the voices that encircled the periphery of the dome singing classics like *O Come all Ye Faithful, O Holy Night,* and *Do You Hear What I Hear?* Ten essential life skills[17] are taught at the SOM. These include concentration, memory, and listening, which will be employed in learning the songs in *The Christ Seed.* Mind maps employ two more of these skills: imagination and reasoning. Adding dreamwork, unlocks another — intuition — for it calls upon the oldest language known to mankind[18], the Universal Language of Mind — pictures — to illustrate each song's meaning. The impact of this work on dreams was clear in Josephine Goffe's dream journal. She writes:

"As a member of the 'choir of angels,' my song of choice for mind mapping was *Silent Night*[20]. The assignment was given October 17, 2010, and we presented the mind maps on November 21, 2010. Between November 8 and November 22, I experienced five dreams about mind maps; four of those dreams were in a four-day period. I actually experienced two dreams about mind mapping in one night. Here are my dream records.

On November 19, 2010, I dreamed:
> *I am making a mind map. I decided that the mind map would be better or more effective if it was in 3D. In order to get the 3D effect I made the map in 3 layers and mounted them on top of each other. I woke up, went back to sleep, and dreamed: The mind map was in 3 parts and it was being shown to an audience as a slide show.*

On November 20, 2010, my dream again was about mind mapping. It is interesting to note that the assignment was for two mind maps. The dream on this night indicated that I had two pieces of paper for my mind map. I dreamed:

*I am making a mind map displayed on 2 pieces of paper.
I decided to show the mind map like a slide show. Paul
M. (student at the completion phase of doctorate of
metaphysics) assisted with the technology of placing the
mind map on the computer.*

On November 22nd I again had a dream about mind mapping. I dreamed:

*I am on the campus of the College of Metaphysics.
Others and myself had performed several activities in the
garden and planted trees in the orchard. I was with one
of the male college students. (I must have become lucid
for I remembered thinking about what understanding
I was building). There were other students building a
large structure on the grounds of the campus.*

I awoke, went back to sleep, and had the following dream:

*I am on the campus of the College of Metaphysics with
a male college student, and we were attempting to paste
the activities we had done on a mind map. We each
had our own mind map. One of the activities that I had
performed, I placed on the lower left of my mind map.
The lower left of the mind map was less populated than
the rest. I realized that I had to identify more activities
in order to populate the lower left portion of the mind
map."*

When I asked Josephine how she regarded mind mapping, she said that it is an intelligent use of the Universal Language of Mind. She saw the dream mind-mapping as symbolic of her mental growth through assembling information for heightened mind function. Josephine identified three intentional activities that fortified the dream consciousness connection between mind mapping the cantata songs and dreaming of mind mapping.

First, as a SOM student, she was studying lesson material on "Dream Awareness". The lesson teaches how the inner level life influences the outer life. It focuses on practices for becoming more aware in dream states.

"Because of this lesson," Josephine said, "I am deliberately attempting to affect my dreams by performing various activities throughout the day." Josephine chose to focus on leadership, patience, gratitude, cooperation, generosity, charisma, and respect. Each day, she selected one of these qualities, periodically resting her mind on its meaning and visualizing the change of vibration she was adding to herself.

Second, nightly meditation harmonized her conscious and subconscious minds.

Third, after writing the next day's date in her dream journal, Josephine said the following affirmation: "I want to wake up from a dream and go back to sleep and continue with the dream."

Because she kept meticulous records, Josephine could trace the connections between deliberate, focused daily disciplines and activities and the five dreams. "During the sleep state, the subconscious mind presented to me where I was placing my attention during the day," she said.

When Josephine linked her conscious dreaming in the day with her subconscious dreaming at night she created the Dream Consciousness Circuit. "Dream" comes from the thinking capacity of the inner minds, working together, to generate desires and to fulfill them. "Consciousness" refers to the interplay of imaging and will that enables existence to be acknowledged and recognized. "Circuit" is the specific path between two points along which signals can be carried. It is the catalyst enabling consciousness to produce a dream. Josephine's experiences exemplify the power of dream study, individually.

The mind maps of all choir members, at varying levels of SOM study, highlight common imagery in the minds of the group. When class members shared their maps with the group, the Dream Consciousness Circuit took on a magnified significance. Placing 15 mind maps of *Hark the Herald Angels Sing* side-by-side gave a very real picture of the thinking of the 15 people who created them. Students created a network, an arrangement of circuits, and the commonalities were brought to light. Those commonalities, drawn as angels, earth and sky, symbols of healing and Christ, revealed the common thought form of the group and the students could see the meaning in the song. The minds of the choir were unified and the group was consciously created, even while they slept.

Rehearsing in Our Dreams

Interestingly, within this group a dual dynamic arose in those studying part-time at one of the branches of the School of Metaphysics in a major U.S. city and those studying full-time at the College of Metaphysics in the countryside of Missouri.

The number of dreams remembered by lead characters who study at college, 187, compared to the number of dreams remembered by lead characters who study at schools branches, 13, points to greater dream recall from those electing full-time study. This is also substantiated by the number of dreams recalled by choir members studying at college, 315, and the number of dreams remembered by choir members studying at schools, 205.

The average dream recall in a week for those living at the college was 3-4 dreams, higher than the average of those participating in the study. The average dream recall in a week for those living in a city was 2-3 dreams, lower than the average.

When the content in dreams is studied, the impact of full-time study and practice becomes clear. Out of 720 total dreams remembered, 404 dreams of them contained no cantata reference. These were dreams like this one:

10-24 Emily's dream
In a big restaurant and lounge. I am serving tables. I taste some of the beers to explain to the customers what they taste like. One is very thick and like syrup. Later I am with a family — a dad and a son. The son and I are eating ice cream together and I ask for lots of chocolate syrup. It starts to drip off the sides.
Later I am at a University looking for something.

The dreams used in this study were recorded between October 1, 2010 and December 18, 2010. To make it easier to note connections between dream content and our common musical work, several of the researchers delineate the characteristics that will define a "cantata dream". These are placed in three categories: 1] People: anyone who is directly associated with the presentation, people portrayed in the Christmas story, even angels. 2] Places: the Peace Dome, the College of Metaphysics, Bethlehem. 3] Things: music, singing, dancing, star of David, **Bible** study, pregnancy. Three hundred sixteen are found to contain at least one of these defined elements.

Dreams involving music are the most common among the dreamers, with 71 including singing, composing or dancing. This would seem to indicate a link between the group's reason to be and their individual dreams. It also indicates something else. Dreams featuring music begin in early October and pick up as the time of performance nears. This seems to point to a Dream Consciousness Circuit link between subconscious thinking (the dreams) and conscious thinking (performance). Here are excerpts from nine of those dreams.

*COMPOSING: 10-6 Charlotte's (choir member, first time soloist) dream
> *I was singing a beautiful song and dancing a floating sort of dance. Another woman there (I did not recognize) remarked that it was a beautiful song. I said, "Yes, I wrote it". I continued to sing some more. Then I said, "It's a John Denver melody, but I wrote these words." (It was the melody to 'Annie's Song.' I don't remember the words I made up.)*

*RECORDING: 10-20 Karen's (choir member) dream
> *Woke up singing "This is my Quest". A small part of the dream that I remember is recording the songs in the Dome with everyone in the group.*

*SINGING: 10-30 Josephine (choir member, soloist) dream
> *I am placing clothing in the washing machine and there are other people using another washing machine downstairs. Karen M. came in with additional clothing — some belonging to Dr. D. Karen and I were singing.*

*PLAYING/SINGING: 11-16 Tad's (portrays Zechariah) dream
*Dr. Pam was playing her harp — Minerva. I was singing
in the dome.*

*REHEARSING: 11-16 Matt's (choir director) dream
*All the cantata members were present in the Peace
Dome, and we were rehearsing the songs for the cantata
while sitting in a circle, I was conducting. After singing
"The Quest" Dr. Barbara said that it was a good day of
rehearsal, and that we should all be getting some rest to
prepare for tomorrow.*

*PRACTICE: 11-21 Katrina's (portrays Elizabeth) dream
*I was rehearsing the Cantata in my dreams all night long.
Running through the whole thing from begining to end
over and over, refining it.*

*PLANS: 12-14 Christine's (choir member, guitarist) dream
*Heather practices a song she will sing and it sounds
pretty good, but is a little out of tune. Elizabeth looks
in a mirror and talks about her future musical plans at
different SOM centers*

*SINGING: 12-14 Pam's (choir member, harmony coach)
dream
*I wrote "singing" in my dream journal for this day. That's
all I remembered.*

*HARMONIZING/IMPROVISING: 12-15 Christine's (choir
member, guitarist) dream
*At one point, me and 4 others (including 1 black man)
sing together. I lead, remembering the words as best I
can and they harmonize. Then we improvise.*

The different ways music appears in the dreams illustrates
the broad range of the demands the cantata places on the class.
Solos, duets, quartets, sextets, choral pieces with harmony, and
instrumentation are featured in the presentation, and people are
stretching, entering new territory and discovering what they
are capable of producing. Their dreams reflect this, offering

them ways to learn and to express any apprehension. Dreaming becomes additional rehearsal time that sharpens their skill without requiring valuable day time out of their schedules.

The most telling statistic so far is that of all the students, 100% remembered dreams during the duration of the class, and all but one person recorded at least one cantata dream.

Most people don't think about group dreaming. Yet on October 24, 75% of the choir members remembered their dreams. This highest dream recall for the cantata class follows a special weekend at the college called the Still Mind Weekend. It is dedicated to silence, fasting, and open-eyed meditation while sitting with a teacher. It is that stillness that makes it easy to receive the inner voice that comes through in our dreams. The consciousness impact of this weekend shows in that 3/4ths of the cantata cast remembered dreams even though less than half of the choir members physically attended the event.

Increasingly, as we branch out past individual dream study to group research, these kinds of connections will be brought to light.

Dream incubation has been practiced in cultures around the world for thousands of years. For SOM students, it describes the intentional planting, by willful action of the Conscious Mind, of a seed idea into Subconscious Mind. (See "Dream Incubation" chapter, page 91.) As a teacher, weaving dream incubation into a group interested in artistic expression is a natural step in evolving the creative mind.

Intuitive research[19] conducted by SOM describes this phenomenon in this way:

> "This one tends to experience creative mind in endeavors with other people. It is through other people that this one becomes aware of how creation works, what it is, what this one has to contribute. It is through the interaction with other people who are thinking, who are in her presence and thinking, that this one is able to experience more of the creative mind than this one does at other times."[20]

This concept is at the heart of interpersonal relationships, and these can be tracked in the dreaming activity.

Instances of connected dreaming and mutual dreaming, the shared dream experience surfaced as dream journals were compared. Memories of attending inner level dream classes and rehearsals convened by their teacher began making themselves known and this is the level of research we expect to document in future cantata classes. Most people don't think about group dreaming. Our expectation is, after participating in a group like this, our students will be awake to a greater reality the rest of their lives.

One student wrote in her dream journal:
> *Special note — I had a roommate (Gerry) sleeping in the bed next to me who said that I was singing in my sleep.*

This student was continuing the practice from her day into her night-time sleep.

By recording their dreams, students were able to track their daytime and night-time experiences. They began to see connections between their thinking and their dreaming, their choices and their dreaming, and their actions and their dreaming. They observed that the dreaming helped them

communicate *subconsciously* between one another, sometimes telepathically, sometimes by occupying the same dream space.

This was emphasized when Tad starred in a dream Laurie had for the first time. These two people had known each other for 10 years, both living on the college campus for most of those, yet Laurie had never remembered a dream about Tad, until December 6, 2010.

Since a nightmare at the age of six woke Barbara, she has invested in the kind of education that can raise a generation without fear. From books like **Interpreting Your Own Dreams: The Six Elemental Thought Forms** *to webinars on time travel and parallel universes, Dr. Barbara O'Guinn Condron is Governor of International Education for the School of Metaphysics and creator/developer of www.dreamschool.org, an online program of dream exploration and study dedicated to creating a global culture that values dreaming.*

Visitations
and Other
Realities

Grief
as an Altered State
of Consciousness

When tragedy strikes, people build memorials. Memorial gardens, statues, places established to remember those who gave their lives or lost their lives. Sometimes those who survive proclaim that we should never forget the disaster.

Never forget the destruction. Never forget those we left behind — or who left us behind. Never forget what happened.

When people die, the survivors often experience an altered state of consciousness. It seems like the veil separating waking physical consciousness from the "other side" dissolves. Those who remain can feel the presence of their departed loved ones. They may have dreams in which those who have died come to them with comforting messages. It seems that the urge to "never forget" is an unconscious plea to  keep the door open to that other world where the spirit lives forever. Dreams give us a clue to this altered state because in that inner realm we can experience life beyond the physical form.

The Tornado

In May of 2011, a tornado struck Joplin, Missouri. It swept through the center of town, leaving a 13-square-mile path of destruction. The city's high school, hospital, and historic Cunningham Park were all wiped out. It killed 160 people. It injured hundreds more. Seven thousand homes and 500 businesses were destroyed.

A month after the tornado, a friend of the School of Metaphysics (SOM) learned about a company called Tom's of Maine that offers funds to not-for-profit organizations for community projects that engage volunteers. Joplin is only a hundred miles from SOM World Headquarters. To help our neighbors, the School of Metaphysics submitted a proposal to build a peace garden in Joplin as a place for comfort and peace, renewal, and resurrection.

The proposed garden was intended not to memorialize those who died in the tornado, but as a place for healing, prayer, and meditation. It was proposed as a gathering place fostering peace and serenity, and to celebrate the generosity of the service of volunteers. The Joplin Peace Garden was intended to embody the cycles of life, celebrating the resolve, dedication, and optimism in the human spirit.

Tragedy often brings with it profound life lessons. In Joplin, people were shaken by the sudden devastation. The tornado gave little warning. For some people, everything they owned was gone in minutes. The lesson of non-attachment is part of the reality of living as spiritual beings in this physical world.

In times of sudden change, those who survive experience conflicting thoughts and feelings. Many people are profoundly grateful that their lives were spared. Often, there is a sense that there is a higher purpose for them to serve. This may be mixed with feelings of guilt, wondering why one's own life or house or business was spared when another's was destroyed. Some people feel remorse or regret about what they could have done to prevent the tragedy, how they should have seen it coming, or what they wished they had said or done (or hadn't said or done) while their loved ones were still alive.

People wonder, "Why me? What is the purpose for this in my life? Is there a meaning beyond my comprehension?"

The people of Joplin recognized that something special occurred after the tornado. Amidst the tragedy arose a profound sense of gratitude. When people experience loss — loss of life, loss of property, loss of physical security — something else is born: awareness of what is permanent. The survivors of the tornado described an awakening within themselves and the community. They were inspired by the love that lasts beyond death and deep appreciation for families, friends, and colleagues.

Miracles

Despite the devastation of homes, businesses, and property, Joplin residents were also struck by a sense of awe, viewing some of the events as truly miraculous. For example, the tornado struck right after the high school graduation. The commencement ceremony that was supposed to take place at Joplin High School was moved shortly beforehand to the other side of town where there was a larger facility. Had the graduation been at the Joplin High School building, many more people would have been killed since that building was right in the tornado's path. Instead, the thousand or so people who attended the graduation were three miles away, safe from the tornado.

Stories like this stimulate people to view their own lives from a different perspective. They recognize that there is a purpose to serve. Some ask themselves, "What do I need to do with my life? How can I improve? In what ways can I give more or become better?" These are some of the blessings that emerge from situations of dramatic change.

That kind of question, the "why?"s are brought to our attention any time there is dramatic change in the physical world. In times of physical change, people's sense of Self is either shaken to the core or strengthened. In Joplin, it became evident that the spirit of the people was fortified. Thousands of volunteers came from miles around, giving time and energy to support and aid. They donated money, clothing, food and service, drawing upon their own resources to clean up debris, to haul off trash, to rebuild and renovate.

I have observed that to be true any time there is a sudden tragedy. It happened with hurricane Katrina; it happened when the Twin Towers were struck on September 11, 2001; it happened with the earthquake that struck Japan in March of 2011. Along with the destruction of property and the loss of human lives, there is also a kind of resurrection of people's spirits.

Gratitude

I hope that people come to realize the beauty in everyday life. I envision a day when people feel free to be open and to express love without waiting for tragedy to strike. I believe that the natural urge to give, to love, to aid, to show affection and gratitude, is stronger than any limitation. We can all learn to give because we want to, to anticipate needs, to look for places to improve ourselves and our communities.

I visited Joplin a couple of months after the tornado struck and met a number of people whose lives were forever changed by the event. The director of the Welcome Center on Highway 44, a rest stop that welcomes travelers into Missouri from Oklahoma, was inspired by the idea of a peace garden as a place for people to come to celebrate the meaning of life and to express gratitude for their loved ones.

I envision a day when people feel free to be open and to express love without waiting for tragedy to strike.

She told us that in the aftermath of the tornado, people coming into Missouri stopped at the Welcome Center to find out where the tornado hit. It became a tourist attraction. To her it seemed like a paradox that something so devastating could bring new people into the community.

She also told us people expressed a kind of intimacy and openness they had previously avoided. When she came to work the day after the tornado she was thrilled to see people who also survived. "I am not a very touchy-feely person," K. said, "but I was so glad to see my friends and co-workers I wanted to hug them! These were people I've known my whole life who I had never hugged before. They were the best and warmest hugs I had ever experienced! People were so grateful to be alive and to find out that their friends and colleagues were alive, too. It taught us not to take anyone for granted."

I hope that people do not wait for destruction or devastation to share such genuine caring and love with their colleagues. What kind of world might we have if everyone expressed openly with one another?

Finding the Good in any Experience

When I was fifteen years old, my father died. At that age, I didn't really understand what was happening. I did not know where he had gone. It was a difficult experience for me and a troubling time in my life. Yet, my memories of my father are not ones of sadness and grief. They are thoughts of profound love. I remember my father as a warm, affectionate, loving person. Those early experiences showed me that love is strong and powerful, and remains beyond death.

Although I only had fifteen short years with my father, the depth of my experience has served me well throughout my life. The goodness of having such a brief period of time with him is that it stimulated me to realize that every moment of life is precious. We should take advantage of it.

When a tornado or car wreck or disease takes the life of a loved one, people experience pain if they have "unfinished business." They mourn the loss of opportunity to resolve what was left undone. They regret the unsaid words, and after death it is too late ... unless they experience after death communication in the dream state.

We never know how much time we have with someone. So right now, in the moment, it is important to express what we want and need to. I hope that all of us learn to live that way.

Security

This applies to any kind of change. Everything in the physical world is in a state of flux. The earth is changing. Shortly after the Joplin tornado, Hurricane Irene killed 43 people on the East

Coast and left 6.4 million people without any electrical power. Two months before the Joplin tornado, a massive earthquake struck Japan. No one knows exactly how many people lost their lives in the earthquake and ensuing nuclear power meltdown, but estimates range from 3,000 – 10,000 people.

With so much uncertainly in the physical world, people find their sense of security can be easily shaken. A mother whose sense of purpose comes from giving to her child might plunge into depression if her child dies. Some people even believe that there is no reason to live when a loved one perishes in a seemingly senseless manner. People who place their security in money become afraid if their investments crash or if they lose their job. They no longer feel safe when something happens to their house or possessions, like those that were destroyed in the tornado.

It is essential for us to learn what is real and lasting, beyond those physical things and experiences, because everything in the physical world changes. Our bodies change. None of us has the same physical body that we had when we were five years old. Most of us do not have the same clothes or cars that we had twenty years ago. So what does provide lasting security?

That security comes from within the self. It stems from our knowledge of how to create.

The Divine Plan

The diagram on page 3 shows how the School of Metaphysics describes the Whole Self and the mind. If you could visualize this triangle being like the cross section of a sphere, then the top of the triangle is like the center of a sphere. At the top of the triangle is LIGHT, which is at the center of who we are. At our center is pure light, or pure awareness.

I understand that we are here to express and manifest our light. This is our purpose in life. That is why we have such a powerful urge to share our love with other people, to express ourselves, and to be creative. Radiant light is our very essence.

The I AM is our individual spark of light. It is our true identity, the Real Self, as it is named in the **Bhagavad Gita**. The mind itself is a vehicle for the expression of the I AM. At the top, or innermost mind, is a Divine Plan in the superconscious mind. The Divine Plan is brought to our attention when we experience miracles. This became apparent to me in meeting and visiting with the people in Joplin. Many people were aware of this superconscious plan working through their lives — forces beyond their control, forces that seemed benevolent when their lives were spared.

For example, the Wildcat Glades Audubon Center in Joplin, Missouri is on the edge of town. It is a beautiful nature center whose mission is simple and elegant: to connect people with nature. The Executive Director said that some of the people who work at the Audubon Center felt guilty that all of their trees were perfectly fine when the 150-year-old trees in Cunningham Park were ripped out of the ground and completely destroyed.

The guilt that she initially experienced very quickly transformed into gratitude when the nature center became a place for Joplin's youth to come receive nature's healing power. They focused on aiding children because more than 60% of Joplin's schools were destroyed or damaged, and thousands of homes and playgrounds were decimated in the 13-square-mile path of the tornado, approximately 30% of Joplin.

When she saw the families who came to the Audubon Center for nature programs, she understood why their trees stood strong and the wildlife lived. Their center became a sanctuary for those in need. "You could tell that these kids had been affected by the tornado when they came in with bandages and cuts. They came to our programs to heal... Nature can be a benevolent force as well as a destructive one."

Resurrection

The School of Metaphysics developed the idea of building a Peace Garden in Joplin as a place for people to experience resurrection. Just as nature can be destructive, like a tornado or a hurricane or an earthquake, it can be nurturing and comforting. Nature is greater than any one of us. It follows cycles. The sun rises and sets. The calm that follows a storm is part of a natural rhythm. Human beings sometimes forget that, thinking that we can dominate everything. Natural disasters can bring to us a sense of humbleness. We can learn that we are here to fulfill our part of a Greater Plan.

In my study and practice of metaphysics I have found that most people have some sense of that. They may not know exactly what their plan is, but they have some idea or feeling that there is a reason for them to be here, a purpose beyond just having a good job, reputation, money, friends and a loving family. Many people believe that there is a destiny for their existence on this earth.

That is why I began to study metaphysics. I wanted to know my destiny. I believed, and have found, that it is possible to know and to fulfill that destiny. That sometimes elusive sense of who you are and why you are here is stored in subconscious mind.

The subconscious mind is the place where you go when you sleep at night, when you are dreaming. It is also the place that you go, as I understand it, after death. This is why it is possible for people who have died to come to you in your dreams and communicate with you. They can comfort you and let you know that they are okay. You may also be able to visit them, to go to the place where they are on "the other side."

This experience of the inner levels of consciousness may be reassuring even when outwardly, consciously, we are mourning a loss. The physical body is the only thing that dies. The spirit lives on. This is one of the great lessons our dreams can teach us.

Dreaming of Eternal Life

When I was 43 years old my husband died of complications of juvenile diabetes. He was only 42. He died on September 10,

2000. Almost exactly a year after that, September 11, 2001, I decided to take that day to commemorate the anniversary of his death and to spend some time by myself in meditation and prayer.

Soon after awakening, I got in my car to drive to my destination. I turned on the radio, and the first thing I heard was, "The second tower has been hit!" I didn't know what was going on, and as I listened to the news I found out about what happened in New York with the Twin Towers. It was a very surreal day. Every place I went, people were walking around like zombies, not knowing what had happened, stunned, in shock.

That night, I had a dream that John (my late husband) was in New York, helping the people who had died in the Twin Towers and I asked him, in a somewhat alarmed voice "Are they okay?"

He lit up with a beautiful, effulgent light. It wasn't like a physical light. It was an amazing, awesome light. His whole face lit up with a beautiful smile, and he said, joyfully, "Yes! They're fine! Once they're out, they're fine!" When he said that, I felt a great "Whoosh!" of exhilaration, like a spirit being released. I knew he meant that once they are out of the body, they are fine. I also received from him the message that the people who were not fine were those of us left in the body, who were struck by grief and shocked.

That experience has stayed with me in a profound way because it gave me a direct experience of the truth of eternal life. It was very healing for me personally to receive communication from my husband in that dream. It was also healing for me as a counselor, as a minister and as a teacher to aid other people who were grieving.

Another reason why that particular dream was so helpful to me is that I grew up in a suburb of New York City. When I tried that day to contact old friends who live in New York, I could not reach them. John's sister and nephew live in Manhattan and I was not able to get in touch with them because all the phone lines were down. So it was very helpful to me to know that I didn't have to have a physical telephone to be able to connect with people.

Dreaming Connects Us

Dreams can give us this experience of mind-to-mind contact. We can practice communicating with other people in our dreams. We do not have to wait for death to bring it to us. One of the challenges we face in society is that we are so in love with technology that we use it as a substitute for the mental and spiritual connection.

Not so long ago, when I was flying somewhere and needed to meet a friend or relative at the airport, I could not just call that person on a cell phone to say, "I'm here; I've arrived." We arranged a meeting place and if either one of us was delayed, we would purposely try connecting with each other telepathically. The person who was late projected a strong thought form to the other. If we listened inwardly, we usually found that we could, indeed, "hear" the other person's thoughts, so we would wait at the appointed place until he or she got there.

How is that possible? Because we exist beyond our physical senses, we can connect with each other in subconscious mind. Most people are not aware of that because the conscious mind is so loud. For many people, there is always some kind of brain chatter going on. It might be thoughts of worry or guilt or thinking of the endless number of things to do. It might be noisy sense stimuli, thoughts of hunger or aches or pains. In addition to the ramblings of the brain, many people walk around with earphones filling the mind with sound: listening to music, or cell phones. We have allowed our conscious minds to be so busy and full of thoughts it makes it much more difficult to listen inwardly.

In order to have peace and security that goes beyond any physical changes, we have to learn to still the conscious mind, to quiet all of that chatter. Then we can receive from the subconscious mind and superconscious mind. This gives us peace. It centers us in the true self, the eternal self.

A Still Mind

At the School of Metaphysics we teach people concentration exercises to cause the conscious mind to become still. We teach people to meditate every day, to listen to the superconscious mind and the Creator. We teach people to listen to dreams, to be aware of the existence beyond the physical body. Paying attention to the inner self enables people to become conscious of a visitation dream, or a dream that can give some kind of guidance.

It is very nourishing when we live that way every day. I think that one reason why people want to remember tragedy and do not want to let it go is that amidst the pain, they experience the reality of existence beyond the body. The veil between the inner and outer mind, between the spirit world and the physical world, seems to lift immediately after the disaster occurs. When masses of people are suddenly killed, the survivors are astonished. The brain chatter ceases. People experience an immediate and profound stillness. That is why on September 11, 2001, people were walking around like zombies. They were shocked.

I heard something similar from the people in Joplin. They said that right after the tornado people were wandering around in a kind of stupor. When a sudden blow produces shock, the conscious mind is arrested. People are not busy thinking. They focus on the present moment, the immediate needs. They function automatically, it seems, almost like robots. It is like the mind becomes blank. We may think of that as a bad thing; however, it allows the subconscious mind to come through, for us to receive the spirits of those who are no longer in their bodies.

When my husband died, it was sudden and unexpected. He was at home and I was just down the block so I was not with him physically at the time of death. In retrospect, I realize that I felt him calling me when he was departing. I was aware of the invisible existence of spirit. That is why a year later I was able to have that visitation dream.

How Dreaming Keeps the Door Open

It helps to keep a dream journal, recording dreams every night, so that when the need arises for these "big" dreams, the mind is already accustomed to listening to the messages from dreams. I wonder sometimes what it must be like for those on "the other side" who want to communicate. Do they watch over us, waiting for us to "answer the phone," that is, to listen to our dreams, so that they can say, "hello"? We can help them by listening!

In the immediate wake of sudden death, people are attuned to the spirit world. Whether awake or asleep, when our conscious brain chatter is silenced, we can hear and feel the existence beyond the physical body. In the weeks and months following my husband's death, I also had waking visitations where I could feel his presence with me. Oftentimes people have such impressions when there is abrupt and unforeseen death. It is like a door is left open and they experience the presence of the loved ones who have died.

Some people are not consciously aware of such contact because they have been taught to believe that it is not possible. People who believe in the possibility of communication with "the other side" pay attention and therefore can more easily receive it. I recently spoke with a woman who longed for a visitation dream from her mother who had recently passed away. She said that she often felt her mother's presence by her side when she was awake. She showed me which side of her body she felt her mother's touch. Her cousin received a visitation dream and asked the mother (her aunt) why she was not visiting her daughter in dreams. "I don't need to," said the mother. "I am with her all the time."

I believe that people want to be able to live with awareness of the subconscious mind as part of their everyday lives. Such experiences are comforting because they open us to a more expanded awareness of who we are. When we have contact with inner level reality, it inspires us to want more. That is why some people want to remember the tragedy, because they think the tragedy is the cause for that inner connection.

The tragedy is not the cause. The cause is that the conscious mind chatter has stopped. People have stopped thinking about countless worries or distractions like "I've gotta go to work, I've gotta make this money, I've gotta get to this place on time, I have to keep up with the Joneses."

At least for a little while, all of that stops.

Tragedy can aid us to connect with what is real, permanent and lasting. Amy Stevens, a hospice worker and mother of three who lives in Joplin, Missouri, wrote an article in the *Kansas City Star* ten months after the tornado. She wrote, in part:

"Why I never want to forget the Joplin tornado.

When the tornado hit, we were faced with children to heal and a home to rebuild so there wasn't time to be immobilized by intense emotions.

Our minds did what they were created to do and our emotions were parceled out in bite-sized doses, some of them being saved for later when the work was done. The work, for my family, is mostly done.

So, almost ten months after the tornado, I find myself experiencing the emotions of this journey more powerfully than I did in the insane days following May 22, 2011."

Amy goes on to describe that the tears that come unbidden at seemingly-odd times are not tears of sadness or grief. They occur when she is moved by what is real.

"It's gratitude.

It's a mind-boggling, knee-shaking awareness of how blessed I am.

It's becoming overwhelmed with the intensity of how much I love them [my family]. How powerfully thankful I am for our life together and that I married him and that I carried them in my body and that I've had them all these years.

And that I still have them today.

So bring it on, unexpected emotions. Remind me of what I have.

Remind me as often as needed to get it through my distracted mind.

Because I don't ever, ever want to forget. I never want to take the ordinary for granted again."[1]

Amy's sentiments are not uncommon. Most of us want to revere life. Dreams can help us to know, not just believe, that something exists beyond this physical body. Remembering our dreams awakens us to the presence of our own spirit and can connect us with people all over the world, in the body or beyond it. Dreams can bring renewal, refreshment, comfort, and peace.

Who Have I Become?

I would like to encourage people to approach any situation of change, or any situation in life that seems troubling or upsetting, as an opportunity to expand awareness. Look for the good in that experience. That means asking oneself, "Who have I become through that experience?"

The subconscious mind stores permanent understanding. A permanent understanding is a virtue or universal truth that seems like second nature. It becomes a part of us. Most people find when they are responding to a crisis, they bring out courage or generosity they didn't know they had. Or they develop acceptance, or compassion, or patience. Those are a few examples of permanent qualities that we either discover or that we build in our character.

Self-growth is the good in the experience. That is why although I am not happy that my father died when I was so young, I appreciate what his early death brought to me. The good I derived from that experience is my awareness that love is permanent and eternal. That understanding served me well when my husband was dealing with life-and-death complications of disease.

Anytime I am willing to respond to something that seems challenging, to walk into a difficult situation with the intention of becoming more, I grow. I emerge from it as a better person. That is the practice of becoming a Whole Functioning Self. The ideal of the School of Metaphysics is to aid any individual to become a Whole Functioning Self. This means that through our experiences we become more virtuous — more grateful, dedicated, devoted, strong, resilient.

The self-development brings the good out of the experience. I hope that you discover the freedom to be all you can be in your dreams, and encourage you to bring that heightened awareness of yourself into your waking life. When we all do that, we will live in a more connected, compassionate, and benevolent world.

The Alpha and Omega

He touched me with his right hand and said: "There is nothing to fear. I am the First and the Last and the One who lives. Once I was dead but now I live — forever and ever. I hold the keys of death and the netherworld. Write down, therefore, whatever you see in visions — what you see now and will see in time to come."
— The **Bible**, *Revelation 1:16-19*

I have known my good friend Hezekiah since he was less than a week old. Our divine friendship has developed over the years. Sometimes he is the student and I am the teacher; sometimes he teaches me and I am his student. A great storyteller, when he was too young to write, Hezekiah used to "dictate" stories. I enjoyed being the scribe, writing down what he said as he narrated.

He appreciated my ability to listen and receive his mental images, writing almost as fast as he could speak. It challenged my powers of concentration to record every word that came from his quick-thinking mind. On the rare occasions that I had to ask him to pause so that I could capture exactly what he said, he patiently waited, indulging my need for more time even though clearly he was ready to continue his tale.

Once Hezekiah was telling a story about a 12-year-old boy who was discovering his calling, bringing to light the mission he had chosen at birth. In one scene, the boy was contemplating his purpose and had many different ideas about what he was to do. His friends and teachers advised him to listen to the first thoughts that came into his mind, but the problem was that his thoughts came into his mind all at once, not one at a time.

When Hezekiah said that, I nodded. That's how thoughts come into my mind too — flashing up all at once, in an interconnected web. Images, experiences, memories, inspirations and stimuli that all come together in one intuitive illumination, not in chronological order. He stopped in his story-telling to discuss with me how frustrated he became when other people didn't get that. I understood. We shared how our Aquarian minds grasp ideas in meaningful constellations, and how sometimes people need us to say more words to connect the dots. We appreciated our common experience. Hezekiah and I have built a friendship on "thinking together," one of our favorite pastimes.

Intuitive thinking is like dreaming. Images come together in a pattern that makes sense to the mind, but to the brain may seem disjointed. Writing this book has been like that. I was going to title this chapter "Epilogue," because it is the final piece of this work, but that's not exactly true. My experience of dreaming and developing my dreaming Self has been more like a patchwork quilt than a linear progression of cause-and-effect situations.

Perhaps even more accurate would be to describe it like a tapestry woven from different colored threads. Trying to explain which thought came first is like trying to separate the threads from the picture they create. Describing the whole picture is more accurate and truthful.

Two nights ago, after concentrating for several days on writing, feverishly trying to finish the book, I had a dream. It was long and involved, but the only part I remembered was the final scene:

I am with a group of people at the School of Metaphysics. There are classes going on. I go downstairs to check the soup/stew I made earlier in the day. It is on the front right burner, and I am dismayed to find that it has simmered too long and most of it has cooked away. There is just enough for one serving, but I had planned for there to be more.

I will share with you how I interpreted the dream. *Food* in a dream is a symbol for knowledge. We hear this in our language when we use the expression "food for thought." While some people have ideas that are "half-baked" (not thought through completely), my dilemma is the opposite: letting ideas simmer or cook for too long. This book has been on the "back burner" since 2008 when I first decided to write it. I have been thinking about it, and collecting knowledge in the form of lectures and presentations I've given, for four years!

Now that I am concentrating on writing, I find that I have more and more ideas that keep expanding. But too much expansion (heat) is not further developing the ideas, it is dissipating them; thus, the food in the dream cooked away until there was not much left to eat. The dream is telling me the stew is done: stop cooking and go eat!

There is a time to expand and a time to contract. I have enough ideas. At this point, it is time to contract, to complete the book so that people can digest the ideas.

A couple of weeks ago, when I also dedicated several days in a row to writing, I had a "big dream." It felt like it went on all night long. There were several scenes. It was partially lucid, and at some points I was aware in the dream that some of the scenes came in-between the longer story, which was an International Association for the Study of Dreams conference.

Here is the dream, with my commentary in parentheses describing my perception of the dream characters:

4/4/2012
First scene:
> *A big ship. A way to aid kids – the letter H. I (we?)*
> *are finding ways for them to heal all four legs of the H.*
> *(in the dream, I have the sense that the H is a healing*
> *vibration.)*

Next scene:
> *S.A. (someone I know from IASD, an artist whose*
> *creativity I admire) and lots of people at a long table. An*
> *outdoor fair. I am with a man. He has a wife from a first*
> *marriage.*

We (the man and I) both agree we are not each other's "one and only." There is probably someone else better for us.

I am in a place, a large room, perhaps a School of Metaphysics branch? The College of Metaphysics? There are two baby grand pianos and a natural wood floor. People (including L., a School of Metaphysics student and teacher who is very passionate and energetic) have re-arranged furniture. I open the blinds, then want to close them so I can take a nap. L. is not too supportive.

Next scene:

I have a date with Dr. M. (A doctor who is very passionate about nutrition and alternative health. I do not know him, just know of him.) I am excited and also feel nervous.

Next scene: (continues the scene with S.A. at the outdoor fair)

At an IASD Conference. I am trying to coordinate with C.S. (one of my students at the School of Metaphysics. She is professional, poised, and disciplined) to get to the meeting. She offers to drive. I don't know what time I'll be returning. I say, "it's okay, I'm sure I can get a ride back." (if she wants to leave before I do.)

I haven't eaten; I say I will just eat some fruit and a hard boiled egg.

Then I am looking for my program book. I see K. (my sister) and P. (a male teacher at the School of Metaphysics. K. and P. have a similar quality which I would describe as being very organized, systematic and disciplined in how they learn, how they live, how they do things.) They seem relaxed, not worried (as I am) about getting to the meetings. I realize K. has never seen or been with me at a conference like this.

There are people walking across a campus. I see them from previous years' conferences.

Next scene:

In-between these scenes, a bizarre dream. It is like a movie scene that I am watching. A man who looks like the actor Christopher Walken, with a huge weapon, like an electric saw. He is battling a young boy (around age 9 or 10) who is treating it kind of like a game. The man saws through the door to a room.

The boy escapes, goes outside. He is building an ice rink, oval and kind of oblong-shaped. At one point he says something about being glad it's not hot outside. He has no coat and likes the cool weather.

Then the man is coming. At this point I am in the dream. He (the boy) and I run. I am terrified. We are hiding by the curb, crouched down by the wheel of a car that is parked by the curb. I realize I could wake myself up.

(Although in the dream I am thinking I should let the dream play out and not stop it by waking up.) I am too scared, though, so I do wake myself up (and then realize later I woke up in another dream, not fully awake in the physical level of consciousness.)

I am thinking in the dream I should really master lucid dreaming; then I wouldn't have to be afraid and would really know that my body is just temporary. I can't fully surrender to it.

I am looking for a symbol/totem that will help. I see the religious symbol that looks like a hand.

Another scene:

Earlier, there is a poster for/about the people who are serving at the conference. K.K. (one of my students who is very physical in his orientation, motivated by how things look and outward expression) has been involved in making it. He remarks on how many people I've influenced over the years and I add, "yes, and the soul growth it has produced" (in myself).

When I awoke, I wrote down the dream, capturing as much detail as I could, although I know there was even more than I have recorded here. It was so profound it kept playing on my mind, and continues to resonate deep within me. The overall impression and theme is about stages of growth in my spiritual development. Where am I in my awareness of myself as spirit? How well do I know, not just believe, that I exist beyond the physical body? And how I am using dreaming in the context of my spiritual education?

The School of Metaphysics approaches dreams not as a "subject," like a class "about dreams" or "about meditation." Rather, it is a developmental process that teaches a student, through practice, how to know him or herself beyond the physical body, through direct experience in the inner levels.

This dream starts out with a scene about healing — meaning whole, or holy — and ends with a scene about soul growth. In-between, the thread that runs through the dream is the ongoing dream conference, an educational setting to learn about dreams from many perspectives (symbolized by the many people in the dream).

There are the two scenes with men I don't know whom I am dating (or about to date). I recognize with one of these men that there is the potential for a deeper relationship with a soul-mate. That symbolizes to me I am harmonizing with aspects of my inner self that are new to me and aware of a desire for more complete union with my inner self.

In the middle there is the nightmarish scene from which I want to escape. *I am aware in the dream* that I can overcome the incredible terror I feel through mastering lucid dreaming. Surrender is the key to dissolving fear. In the dream itself I know I need more practice, and when I ask for a totem for help, the dream gives me an immediate response, clear and definite.

To understand it, I needed to do some research, starting with looking up the religious symbol/totem of the hand. I have seen that symbol before and recognized it in my dream, but consciously (and in the dream also) did not know what it was called, or its religious source.

That portion of the dream was partially lucid, with a mystical quality to the hand symbol that I can only describe with a word frequently used by C.G. Jung: numinous.

Researching the hand revealed some amazing links among what, at first, seemed like different elements of the dream.

The symbol is called a "hamsa" which means five. Interestingly, the letter H, which appeared in the first scene of the dream as a healing symbol, is the fifth letter of the Hebrew alphabet, and in Hebrew it is appears twice in the name Yahweh, YHWH or God.

The letter H in Hebrew means "in general universal life, clarity, the breath of existence, the act of feeling and willing, transcendental knowledge, and universal magnetism. It also is related to the elements; in YHWH the first "H" signifies air, or breath, and the second "H" signifies earth."[1]

This makes sense. Bringing my thoughts to earth, grounding them, is an integral part of my soul work this lifetime.

In my research I discovered that in Hebrew the symbol itself for "H" looks like a window, "The letter stems from a root that means 'to breathe' in the sense of allowing air and light. To see and to breathe are two vital aspects of life. A window allows light and air to come in. It is an opening by which the light outside can reach us."[2]

Clearly my subconscious mind was revealing something unknown to my conscious mind by using the "H" as a healing symbol in the dream. What is more healing than light and breath?

The definition of the "H" as universal life relates to the meaning of the hamsa. The hamsa does not belong to one religion. It is a symbol used in Judaism, Christianity, Hinduism, Islam, Buddhism, Shamanism, and Jainism. Its origins are unknown but it was used by the ancient Phoenicians as a protective symbol for a Middle Eastern Goddess.

Sometimes the hamsa is called the hand of Miriam (sister of Moses and Aaron) and sometimes it is called the hand of Fatima, daughter of Mohammed. The hamsa hand has always been associated with a female entity offering protection from evil and misfortune. In the Jewish religion, the Jewish hamsa hand also symbolizes the Hand of God.

As an interfaith minister, and a person raised without a formal religion this lifetime, it makes sense that a religious totem in my dream would be universal rather than one associated with a particular faith.

So what does all of this mean?

The potency of the religious totem/symbol got my attention. It came in the part of the dream that was like a nightmare, with the menacing man of whom I was afraid. In the dream, I had some awareness that I could wake myself up but should not, because I would be avoiding the fear rather than surrendering to something greater that lay beyond:

Then the man is coming. At this point I am in the dream. He (the boy) and I run. I am terrified. We are hiding by the curb, crouched down by the wheel of a car that is parked by the curb. I realize I could wake myself up.

(Although in the dream I am thinking I should let the dream play out and not stop it by waking up.) I am too scared, though, so I do wake myself up (and then realize later I woke up in another dream, not fully awake in the physical level of consciousness.)

I am thinking in the dream I should really master lucid dreaming; then I wouldn't have to be afraid and would really know that my body is just temporary. I can't fully surrender to it.

I am looking for a symbol/totem that will help. I see the religious symbol that looks like a hand.

Why this symbol? In addition to the universal character, a hand symbolizes purpose. Human beings use their hands to write, to create, and to work. The word man, which comes from the

Sanskrit word "manu," meaning thinker, is related to the word "manual," as in manual labor, or handiwork.

The number "5" (which hamsa means) signifies causing change through reasoning. In the physical world, death is a change, perhaps the most complete change. I understand death in a dream to symbolize change. In this dream my fear of death precipitated the call for a religious symbol or totem for help. So, although all of these details were not a part of the dream, they all came together in the picture/symbol/totem of the hamsa, hand of God, related to a feminine goddess.

Feminine. Yielding. In the **Bible**, when Mary discovers that she is with child, and that the father of the child is God, the angel comes to her and says, *"Do not fear, Mary. You have found favor with God ... The Holy Spirit will come upon you and the power of the Most High will overshadow you. ... nothing is impossible with God."* Mary completely surrenders, saying, *"I am the servant of the Lord. Let it be done to me as you say."* (*Luke 1:30 – 37)* This feeling of complete surrender to spirit, believing in and expecting a miraculous transformation, was what I wanted, but knew I didn't have, in the dream. I wanted to wake myself up to escape the fear, knowing at the same time that if I had mastered lucid dreaming I could just give myself completely to the change (death) and go beyond fear.

This is where the tapestry becomes even more intertwined. Death and resurrection has been a theme for me this lifetime. Although I have never had a near-death experience, I have been in the presence of loved ones who existed in states in-between life and death, living for awhile in a medically-induced limbo. Learning how to relate to people I loved whose consciousness was not always fully present made my own waking existence dream-like. Sometimes it was like being in an altered state of consciousness. It heightened my experiences of telepathy, clairvoyance, remote healing, and visitations. In pondering the role of death in my lifetime, I have come to the conclusion that it has magnified my awareness of eternal life.

Reflecting on my upbringing, I can see how being raised without a religion stimulated me to ask questions about life and death, what is real and what is imaginary, and even more fundamentally, "Who am I?" I was taught as a child that death is the end. When you're dead, you are dead. Gone. No more existence. You exist in a physical body, and when the body dies, that's it. From the perspective of myself as a physical being, the death of my father when I was only 15, and my husband when I was 43, was a great loss. From the perspective of myself as a soul, these deaths were a kind of "wake-up call," inspiring me to long for existence beyond the flesh.

When my father was diagnosed with cancer I was only seven. The doctors thought he would die within a year. Through desire, willpower, allowing himself to become a guinea pig for then-experimental medical treatments, self-hypnosis, and dietary change, my father lived for eight years beyond the original prognosis. Most of the time the cancer was in remission and I experienced my father as a loving, affectionate person.

My parents thought that my sisters and I were too young to understand, so we never really talked about death, the fact that he might be dying or what would happen when he died. I don't even remember being told that he had cancer until I was about 12 or 13. We certainly never discussed our feelings about his illness or his future. My parents did their best to show courage and to give us a good life without troubling us with (in their minds) negative emotions. So I felt a great discord between the words my parents said and the emotions of fear, sadness, and distress that I absorbed from them. I was quite telepathic, so I am sure I received their thought-form-images without having a way to interpret correctly what was happening.

In the last two years of my father's life, the medical procedures and experiments took their toll. He was increasingly drugged-up on medications and shortly before he died endured a surgical procedure to remove his pituitary gland. After that, the body lying in the bed didn't even look like my father any more. His mind was definitely elsewhere. Again, I had no way to interpret what was happening in my conscious mind. I had no spiritual grounding or explanation. It felt to me like I was living in a kind of netherworld myself.

Ironically, I was watching the movie *Harold and Maude* (a film about funerals, death and life) with a group of kids at the moment my father's consciousness left the physical body. I was away from home on a cross-country tour. Since we had not talked about my father's impending death, when I learned that he died I felt numb. People told me I should cry, but I couldn't because I just felt ... nothing.

There was no funeral. I never saw his body. By the time I flew home from the tour, the body was gone from the house. It was a very strange experience. In my brain I had information that he died, but I didn't really know what that meant. It was hard for me to admit that he was gone. I had not said goodbye. There was no closure, and it was difficult to absorb the truth that he had, indeed, exited my life. It seemed like there was no place to rest my mind. Where did he go? I couldn't feel him, and had not really been able to feel his presence for the last year of his life. It took me many years and much experience with dreaming and waking visitations to understand what was happening back then.

My early experience of death was that it happens in degrees. It is not black and white: one minute you are alive, and the next you are dead. It was more like a gradual slipping away of consciousness, a kind of grey and (in the case of my father) murky experience of being somewhere in-between.

Although I was not conscious of it at the time, I am certain that on a soul level, I chose to marry a man whose fate was similar to my father. He died young. He allowed himself to become a medical guinea pig and also went through a several-year period of being healthy and wholly functioning at times, while in-between life and death at other times. The story of my journey with John through the medical world is told in the book **Karmic Healing**.[3]

The difference in my experience with John and my father was the depth of understanding I had gained of how to interpret inner-level energies. As a child and young teenager, I had no way to explain what was occurring. I felt as if I was walking through a dream, at times, and thought that I must be crazy. By the time I was married, I had practiced spiritual disciplines for years. My husband and I met through the School of Metaphysics and were purposeful about our use of telepathy, mutual dreaming, meditation, and other ways of consciously accessing subconscious realities. So when John was partly conscious and partly delirious from prescription drugs, I could still communicate with him telepathically. I was able to reach him in dreams even when we were separated physically, and after his death. By then, I knew I was not crazy and actually more lucid and alive than ever.

> *The more lucid we are when awake, the more awake we can be in dreams. The more we sleep through life, the more unconscious we are in dreams.*

From my current vantage point, I view death as a transition, a progressive movement of consciousness rather than a final slamming of a door. Learning to become lucid in dreams seems to be a related experience. It is a matter of degree rather than "either-or" or "on-off." I have had dreams that were partially lucid. I have also been in touch with subconscious existence while awake in physical reality. I am beginning to view all of life in degrees of lucidity. The more lucid we are when awake, the more awake we can be in dreams. The more we sleep through life, the more unconscious we are in dreams.

Learning to embrace transformation is the work I am doing now. In the **Bible**, Paul says, "I die daily." Sometimes this means surrendering my attachment to ideas, to physical desires, or to people, places, and things. Letting go of ego attachments can be challenging. I believe my dream is telling me that lucid dreaming is the key to learning how to surrender to change, to fully give the self up to a higher Source, to know God.

There is nothing to lose, except my own limitations.

This brings me to my soul assignment. As a young child, one of the many futures I imagined for myself was being a diplomat and ambassador. Little did I know that this would take form in being an ambassador between the inner and outer worlds! In fact, when my mother was in a near-comatose state after suffering a massive stroke, my sisters depended on me to translate her garbled speech. The stroke damaged the connections in her brain that enabled her to find intelligible words to convey meaning. She said words that sounded like nonsense. And yet, I was able to understand what she was saying. With a still mind, I telepathically received her mental images and could then say the correct words, which she affirmed by vigorously nodding "yes" when I had it right. It was a parting gift I could give to her and to my sisters in the last week of her life.

In Mayan astrology, my galactic signature is White Galactic Worldbridger. The essence of Worldbridger is one who bridges the worlds between the seen and unseen worlds, the physical world and the afterlife. The assignment for a White Worldbridger is to understand eternal life through death, to learn how to surrender attachment to the physical form and to know the freedom of the spirit. I have found that most Worldbridgers also serve as guides to aid people cross over from life to death or to navigate the in-between waters of schizophrenia and other so-called mental illnesses.

"*White Worldbridger* is shown on the glyph as a yin-yang split between life — and the afterlife. ... A line runs down the center and within it is an eyelet, a portal through to death — perhaps that beam of light described as the passage between earth and ether existences. On the other side, there is only space: emptiness or a liberated expanse, depending on your fear level of entering it."[4]

Can you see the resonance here with the "H" as a symbol meaning an open window that lets light in?

"*White Worldbridger* celebrates the act of dying, of leaving the temporal world for the eternal one. It teaches us, while alive and well, to expose ourselves to any fears we have of death, of apparent endings. It asks us to bridge our experience here on earth with heaven — now — in anticipation of an eventual death, as well as to honor that the open space of the afterlife is in our every inhalation, in the small separation between us and those we love. We can bring that world of peace and divinity to our lives, letting toxin and obstruction die away from our bodies to make room for infinite life force. *White Worldbridger* lives in both elements, life and death, recognizing the renewal of cycling between.

White Worldbridger is a strong antidote to the current preoccupation with extending human lifespan. The Maya strongly associated dying with rising to the great god in a higher plane of consciousness. The demand on a human body in that culture was great — a constant state of self-reliance for food, water sources, survival through procreation, as well as serving the ruling lord. The relief of rising out of the corporal existence into an etheric realm was palpable, prayed for. Death, then, was a celebration: if a loved one died, they were assured more freedom and ease, as well as being an anchor in the afterlife for the rest of the family's passage.

In modern life ... We are afraid to die and give up this material amassing, these things we claim to own, people we lean into for love. It's not bad, this global hang up, not a sin. It's just paralyzing, a state of inner confusion and fear. So the White Worldbridger is an invitation to break this perception forever and reintroduce death as necessary, graceful and liberating.

... Death is a return to light, so if you are in discomfort, see it lessen – lighten. If you are burdened, again feel death as a means for the weight to rise — be lighter. Experience the endings around you as a means to ascend heavenward, a metaphor for liberation, not loss."[5]

This primal essence, the need to know the liberation of the spirit, was highlighted in my hamsa-hand dream.

Even more interesting, when I was looking through my dream notebook, I discovered a dream I had had about a month earlier with a very similar message. I had not paid much attention to this dream and had forgotten I even had it. Thank God I wrote it down, so that I could heed it when I was ready to hear it!

3/8/2012   full moon dream

I am walking around a college building, dorm. There is a guy I am attracted to; he might be attracted to me also. He is looking through my purse. I hope there is nothing in there that is embarrassing. I tell him a guy should know a girl really well before looking through her purse.

Somewhere in the dream I realize I want to get better at lucid dreaming. I feel embarrassed that I don't have much proficiency with it. I think of L.V. (someone I know from IASD who is a prolific lucid dreamer with skill in precognition, clairvoyance, and remote viewing.) Then I decide to ask a teacher. I ask my teacher — she says, "Can you visit me?" I say, "Well, I can set the intention but can't guarantee I can do it." She seems surprised. Then I realize it is my mother.

Earlier, in the college/dorm setting, a few of us are sitting in a room. There are kids who are coming down a hall we can't see. They come into a room, and when they do, they change and their clothes change, by jumping or turning. Like it is magic or something. The teacher comes in behind us. He seems stern. He says we are not supposed to see it — like it is a secret only for those who know how to do it.

Why did I not remember this dream or pay attention when I first had it? Apparently, my desire to practice lucid dreaming was not strong enough. Or my doubts were stronger than my desire, as shown by my comment to my teacher when I say,

> *Desired change is the key to a purposeful existence.*

"Well, I can set the intention but can't guarantee I can do it." I have had some experience with lucid dreaming but do not consider myself a frequent lucid dreamer. Admittedly, I have had some prejudices, because some of the students I know who can easily lucid dream are people who I view as being ungrounded, who tend to get lost in their imaginations in physical waking reality and who often are not very practical thinkers. I learned this kind of judgment from my mother, who valued scientific proof, who was responsible, practical, and did not give much credence to intuition. Prior to the hamsa dream, I did not have a strong purpose for putting forth effort to practice lucid dreaming.

"Desired change is the key to a purposeful existence." I read this years ago in the novel **Hu Man** written by Jerry Rothermel[6], and for quite awhile I used it as a daily affirmation. It often runs through my mind. Desired change provides motivation. Before the hamsa dream, my attitude toward lucid dreaming was akin to wishful thinking — it would be nice if I could do it, but is it really worth devoting my time to practice? Now I have a passion to master this skill. In the dream I could imagine the freedom of completely surrendering to the Real Self, eliminating the fear of death.

It was the same feeling I had when I dreamed that John died, and the visitation dream when he was helping those who died in the Twin Towers. In this recent dream I was on this side of the door, the physical ego/physical body/fear-laden side. I want to cross over, to know the exhilaration of eternal life, to know God, without having to die physically.

And now another thread to the tapestry ...

At my first IASD conference, I attended a panel on lucid dreaming in which Robert Waggoner told the story of his development in becoming a prolific lucid dreamer. He spoke of a simple exercise taught by Carlos Castaneda (who, by the way, was a White Worldbridger.) Concentrate on your hands before going to sleep while visualizing and affirming with clear expectation an intention to see your hands in your dream. When you see your hands, you will know in the dream that you are dreaming.

Hmm ... I wonder if the hamsa hand in my dream could also be referring to this exercise?

After attending Robert Waggoner's presentation, I was somewhat embarrassed, as in the dream I just related, because I had learned this exercise years ago as a School of Metaphysics student. I had done it regularly for awhile, with sporadic success, and then gave up. I recognized that I was not diligent in training myself to the best of my capabilities, and therefore, in my own estimation, had fallen short.

That night, I decided to put the hand exercise into practice. I spent 20 minutes or so concentrating on my hands, allowing my mind to rest on the desire/ intention of seeing my hands in my dream, expecting that when I saw my hands I would know I was dreaming and become lucid.

Well ... that night I saw my hands in my dream, realized I was dreaming and then started to FLY with a great whirlwind of motion and excitement and energy. I felt my kundalini rise. It was greatly exhilarating and in my dream I shouted "Robert Waggoner! I'm dreaming!! I have to tell you!!" I shouted loudly for awhile, while flying with the great feeling of exhilaration. Unfortunately, my excitement and lack of emotional control woke me up, so the dream was not too long. When I awoke, I thought, "Oh, my! I probably disturbed Robert's sleep shouting like that, since he lucid dreams so often maybe I interrupted his dream!"

I was embarrassed enough by the thought that I emailed Robert Waggoner to apologize in case I had interrupted his sleep, and to thank him for reminding me of this simple practice for lucid dreaming.

This happened in 2008, the same year I decided I was going to write this book on **Intuitive Dreaming**. Now that the book is off the back burner and will have finished cooking by the time you read this, I have one more thread to unravel.

At the beginning of the book I spoke about a friend and college classmate who told me to keep a dream journal as a way to remember my dreams so that I could use the imagery to write poetry. At the same time, in the same college program, I was introduced to the poetry of Robert Frost. A line from one of his poems has stayed with me, as a mantra, since I read it in 1977:

"It's knowing what to do with things that counts."

I have never recalled the entire poem, "At Woodward Gardens," just that one line. It echoes in my mind when I hear people debate esoteric ideas without having a clue as to what they are going to do with them. In a college philosophy class, hearing such a debate, I remember having an out-of-body experience, watching the abstract ideas going back and forth like a tennis match. All of a sudden, I couldn't hear what anyone was saying. The discussion was drowned out by a white noise in my mind, above which I heard, loudly, a voice like the one I've heard in the Voice dreams. The voice said, "What's the point?" It drew my attention to the urgent need for there to be a purpose, some use, for ideas.

It's knowing what to do with things that counts.

Before now, I haven't really known what to do with lucid dreaming, other than enjoying the experience or being entertained. Without some practical application, it has not seemed worth my time to focus on its practice beyond the rudimentary time I spent learning how to do it. Investment is important to me. If I am going to spend time with something, or someone, I want the effort to pay off. As it says in the **Bible**, "Why spend your money for what is not bread, your wages for what fails to satisfy?" — *Isaiah 55:2*

Like my student K.K. pointed out in the last scene of the long dream I recounted at the beginning of this chapter, I have devoted my adult life to aiding other people and to my own soul growth. This is worth my investment.

In the field of metaphysics people can get lost in subconscious experiences, playing with them the way some people use drugs, going around in circles without making any difference in themselves or the world. Applied metaphysics is different. It needs to be grounded, bringing air to earth (as in the symbol of the two H's in the name of God, YHWH). For me, having a purpose for what I think and what I do is of utmost importance.

Until I had that dream of surrender, my purpose for lucid dreaming was weak. Now it is strong.

They say that one picture is worth a thousand words. I would say that one dream is worth a thousand pictures! If one image, a hamsa hand, can bring together the past, present, and future; bring to light the interconnection of karma, dharma, and destiny; stimulate a deep recognition of what it feels like to liberate spirit from the prison of the flesh; and evoke a lifetime's yearning to know God, then just imagine what other doors a dream can open.

Godspeed as you journey through the magical world of dreaming.

About the Author

Laurel Clark devotes her life to humanitarian service through teaching, writing, counseling, and interfaith ministry. She has been a teacher with the School of Metaphysics since 1979 and currently serves as President. She holds a Doctorate of Divinity and Doctorate of Metaphysics.

An accomplished speaker, Laurel often gives lectures to civic, professional and social organizations, corporations, universities, hospices and hospitals on the application of Universal Law for more effective living. She has appeared on radio programs around the world, educating people about the importance of dreams for fulfilling their life purpose and understanding the Self.

In addition to books published by SOM Publishing, Laurel is a contributor to the **Encyclopedia of Sleep and Dreams, Weaving Dreams in the Classroom**, and has numerous articles published both online and in print.

She is writing a book of metaphysical fables for dreamers of all ages.

About the Artists

Illustrating the ethereal quality of a dream can be a challenge. I want to thank the following people for receiving, imagining, and translating my dream images into print through their artistry.

Cover Art: Joseph Leaderbrand
Joseph has been an active dreamer and visionary since he was young. He seeks to understand the workings of the universe and connects with his life purpose by bringing these visions into the physical world in hopes they will bring a sense of peace, wisdom, and unity. Joseph is a student of the School of Metaphysics in St. Louis, Missouri.

Joseph tells this story about the cover: "After talking with you about incubating a dream image, a night or so later I awoke to a lucid vision. All in a flash, I was in the sky, floating, when suddenly, I look up and my field of perception was engulfed by the tremendous brilliance and soothing rays of the moon. It was as if it were right in front of me. I was then pulled backwards over a vast seascape of intermixing blues and greens to a patch of grass underneath a cedar-like tree where I stood peacefully gazing. I awoke and my first thought was about this book cover." He is also the artist for the illustrations on pages 70, 133, and 189.

Layout and Design: Karen Mosby
A graduate teacher at the College of Metaphysics, Karen expresses her creativity through graphic design, cooking, crafts, and photography. She photographed the illustrations on pages 98, 107, 119, and 178.

Laura Atkinson (p. 15, 116)
Laura lives in Rhode Island and is a member of the IASD and the World Dreams Peace Bridge. She says of her work, "As a former photojournalist, I have been exploring the links between art, visual therapy, and the realities of the dream state for many years. My work, a deeply personal exploration of my own dreams, jars the viewer with its beauty of light interplay, form, and design. In my fine art photography, I take an organic approach in creating recognizable images that strike a resonant chord. Making photos is a quietly hidden metaphor for the ever-changing fluidity of our dreams and frailty of beauty, a tangible memoir that everything is not always as it appears to be."

Gay Foltz (p. 114-115)
Gay Foltz started carving under the tutelage of her uncle Rey Bjurstrom and apprenticed with him before developing her own unique style. Gay's repertoire includes cats, dogs, moons, suns, rabbits, crows, flying pigs, dragons or any other creature you or she can imagine.

Gay's work has been featured on HGTV's *"That's Clever"*, in *"Country Folk Art"* magazine, and *"Chip Chats"* magazine. She is a juried member of the Pennsylvania Guild of Craftsmen. Her studio has been an integral part of The Village Artisans Gallery since it opened in 1995.

Oksana Gritsenko (p. 16, 159)
Oksana is a student at the School of Metaphysics in Palatine, Illinois. She was born in Tashkent, Uzbekistan and moved to the US in 1998. Oksana has been studying art since she was nine years old, with her first education and career in Fine Arts and Design.

Kevin Hay (p. 31)
A former student and director at the School of Metaphysics, Kevin designs custom murals for homes, schools, and public buildings. He originally designed this for Laurel's first book **Love Has Many Faces** and it appears in the book **Dharma: Finding Your Soul's Purpose**.

Scott Hilburn (p. 96, 113)
Scott is a student at the College of Metaphysics who dreams of making films to uplift the consciousness of humanity. He is passionate about learning and using every opportunity in this physical world for becoming a creator.

Veneza Marquez (p. 13, 77, 91, 138, 209)
Veneza Marquez has practiced the creation of art since childhood. She has explored various media as a means of developing her consciousness and continues to share her inspirations with others. She is a graduate from the First Cycle of Lessons at the School of Metaphysics. She is now pursuing a career as a massage therapist.

The illustration on page 29 is a composite of a drawing of the World Trade Center by Veneza Marquez and a computer design of the "spirit" by Teresa Martin.

Teresa Martin (p. 13)
A graduate of the School of Metaphysics, Teresa Martin is an author, creative designer, and a teacher of mind. She holds all of the degrees offered by the School of Metaphysics.

Benjamin David Pettingill (p. 36, 45, 91, 145, 195)
Benjamin David Pettingill studied at John Herron School of Art, earned his Bachelor of Arts from Ball State University, and recently received the Respondere from the School of Metaphysics. His dream is to create an animated cartoon series.

Notes

Introduction
1. Universal Language of Mind is a language of symbology. The name is a copyright of the School of Metaphysics.
2. Christine Madar, ed. **The Moon's Effect on Dreams** (Windyville SOM Publishing, 2008).
3. http://www.wfyi.org/dreamtime

What is a dream?
1. Barbara O'Guinn Condron, **The Dreamer's Dictionary** (Windyville, MO: SOM Publishing, 2005).
2. E. W. Kellogg, III, *"Paranormal Phenomena FAQ,"* retrieved from the International Association for the Study of Dream website, http://www.asdreams.org/telepathy/faq_paranormal.htm

Inner Level Communication
From a paper presented at the International Association for the Study of Dreams PsiberDreaming Conference, 2008.
1. Elisabeth Kubler-Ross, **On Death and Dying** (New York, NY: Macmillan, 1969).
2. Raymond A. Moody, Jr., **Life After Life** (Covington, GA: Mockingbird Press, 1975).
3. *Diagram of Mind and Levels of Consciousness*, School of Metaphysics Study, copyright 1976.
4. Laurel Clark, **Karmic Healing** (Windyville, MO: SOM Publishing, 2000).

Messages From Your Soul
Adapted from a lecture given in Indianapolis in 1995
1. Kubler-Ross, **On Death and Dying**.
2. *"Dalai Lama Offers Words of Wisdom About Happiness,"* Hamilton, NY, USA, 23 April 2008, Media-Newsswire.com, retrieved from http://www.dalailama.com/news/post/218-dalai-lama-offers-words-of-wisdom-about-happiness
3. Laurel Clark, **Dharma: Finding Your Soul's Purpose** (Windyville, MO: SOM Publishing, 2004).

Friends, Strangers, Soul Mates, and Other Dream Characters
1. Pat Ballard, *"Mr. Sandman,"* 1954.
2. *Plato's "Symposium,"* retrieved from http://www.classics.mit.edu/Plato/symposium.html
3. http://www.dreamschool.org

Beyond Edgar Cayce
Adapted from a presentation given at the 2010 IASD Conference in Asheville, NC
1. http://www.edgarcaye.org
2. Barbara O'Guinn Condron, ed., **The Work of the Soul** (Windyville, MO: SOM Publishing, 1996).
3. Barbara O'Guinn Condron, ed., **First Opinion** (Windyville, MO: SOM Publishing, 1998).
4. Daniel Condron, **Permanent Healing** (Windyville, MO: SOM Publishing, 1992).
5. Laurel Clark, **The Law of Attraction and Other Secrets of Visualization** (Windyville, MO: SOM Publishing, 2007).
6. http://www.som.org

The Voice-Over Dream
Adapted from a presentation given at the 2011 IASD Conference in the Netherlands.
1. *"'Voice' of Dreams Called Superior,"* New York Times, October 20, 1937, retrieved from http://www.nytimes.com/books/97/09/21/reviews/jung-lecture3.html
2. http://www.younglivingsuccess.com/essential_oil_kits/
3. C. G. Jung, *"Individual Dream Symbolism in Relation to Alchemy,"* in C. G. Jung, Dreams, translated by R.F.C. Hull (Princeton, NJ: Princeton University Press, 1974), 161.

Dream Incubation: Ancient Science and Modern Art
1. Laurel Clark, *"School of Metaphysics Approaches to Dream Incubation,"* in D. Barrett and P. McNamara (eds.), **Encyclopedia of Sleep and Dreams** (Santa Barbara, CA: Greenwood Publishers, 2012).
2. C.A. Meier, **Healing Dream and Ritual: Ancient Incubation and Modern Psychotherapy.** (Daimon Verlag, 1989. Originally published in German, 1949, and translated into English under the title Ancient Incubation and Modern Psychotherapy, 1967).
3. Henry Reed, **"Dream Incubation: A Reconstruction of a Ritual in Contemporary Form**," Journal of Humanistic Psychology, Vol. 16, No. 4 (Fall 1976): 53 – 69.

Dream Inventions, Inspiration, and Insight
Adapted from a lecture given on a national tour in 2008 – 2009
1. *Dream Insights, Inventions, and Intuition*, (SOM Productions, 2010,) CD.
2. *10 Powers of Dreaming*, (SOM Productions, 2006,) CD.
3. Alex I. Askaroff, *"Elias Howe, Master Engineer,"* retrieved from http://www.sewalot.com/elias_howe.htm

4. Deirdre Barrett, *"The 'Committee of Sleep,' a study of dream incubation for problem solving,"* Dreaming, Vol. 3, No. 2, (1993), retrieved from http://www.asdreams.org/journal/articles/barrett3-2.htm

5. Paul Strathern, **Mendeleyev's Dream: The Quest for the Elements** (New York, NY: Thomas Dunne Books, 2000).

6. *"Famous Dreams,"* retrieved from http://www.dreaminterpretation-dictionary.com/famous-dreams-6.html

7. *"Madame C. J. Walker,"* retrieved from http://www.blackinventor.com/pages/madame-walker.html

8. Deirdre Barrett, **The Committee of Sleep** (New York: Crown Publishing Group, 2001).

Extraordinary Dreams from Ordinary People

1. Jackie Gaskins, www.VirtuousGirlsforGod.com
2. Amy Brucker, www.amybrucker.com and www.growyourlifework.com
3. http://www.ld4all.com/forum/viewtopic.php?t=34373
4. pasQuale Ourtane-Krul, www.ld4all.com
5. Roberta Beach Jacobson, www.RobertaBeachJacobson.com
6. Lindsay Vanhove, www.dreamingglobalillumination.com/lindsay-vanhove/
7. Yaina Cantrell, www.silverliningentertainment.biz
8. Curtiss Hoffman, *"The Gilgamesh Cantata: A Personal Exploration of Dreams and Music,"* first published in *Dream Network Journal* Vol. 30 No. 4, (2011) pgs. 12 – 14. For more information about Dream Network visit www.DreamNewtwork.net
9. Gay Foltz, www.villageartisansgallery.com/gay_foltz.htm
10. World Dreams Peace Bridge, www.worlddreamspeacebridge.org
11. Laura Atkinson, www.camerawilltravel.com
12. Laura Pallatin, www.wiyof.com

Day Residue

1. Parapsychological Association Frequently Asked Questions, retrieved from http://archived.parapsych.org/faq_file1.html#7

That Recurring House Dream
Adapted from a presentation given at the 2009 Chicago IASD Conference

Inception

1. www.abcnews.go.com/Entertainment/inside-inception-christopher-nolans-dream-world-exist-real/story?id=11174201

The Dream Consciousness Circuit
Presented at the 2011 IASD conference in The Netherlands
1. www.peacedome.org
2. School of Metaphysics World Headquarters
3. *"Ode"* by Arthur O'Shaughnessy (1844-1881)
4. *Universal Peace Covenant*, www.peacedome.org
5. Hezekiah Condron
6. Heather Hunt
7. Charlotte Crabaugh
8. Karen Mosby
9. Ariadne Conner
10. Diana Kenney
11. Ariadne Conner
12. Golbahar Dadyan
13. Ryan Jones
14. Global Lucid Dreaming Experiments, www. dreamschool.org
15. *Dream Consciousness Diagram* by Dr. B. Condron, published at www.dreamschool.org, SOM, May 2011.
16. **The Mind Map Book** by Tony Buzan with Barry Buzan, 1996, Penguin Group
17. Ten essential life skills are outlined in **Master Living** by Dr. Barbara Condron, SOM Publishing, Nov. 2005.
18. oldest known cave painting is at Chauvet Cave, dated to 30,000 BC, Paul Martin Lester, **Visual Communication with Infotrac: Images with Messages**, Thomson Wadsworth, 2005
19. For more on Intuitive Research conducted by the School of Metaphysics, **Work of the Soul** (1996) and **First Opinion** (1998) by Dr. Barbara Condron, **Dharma: Your Soul's Purpose** (2004) and **The Law of Attraction and Other Secrets of Visualization** (2007) by Dr. Laurel Clark, **Permanent Healing** (1992) by Dr. Daniel Condron, all published by the School of Metaphysics.
20. Intuitive Research file, #(2009-10-31-BGC-07), School of Metaphysics.

Grief as an Altered State of Consciousness
1. http://www.kansascity.com/2012/03/13/3489371/why-i-never-want-to-forget-joplin.html#storylink=cpy

The Alpha and Omega
1. "The Hebrew Alphabet, explanation of the letters, also in relation to the tree of life," retrieved from www.soul-guidance.cm/houseofthesun/treeoflifeletters.html
2. Ibid.

3. Clark, **Karmic Healing**, op. cit.
4. http://resonanttruth.com/2012/01/white-worldbridger-tribe-celebrated-june-13-25-2010/
5. Ibid
6. Jerry L. Rothermel, **Hu Man** (Springfield, MO: SOM Publishing, 1982).

Bibliography

The primary resource I used for this book is my own dream journal. This list includes other books and websites used for research. There are many other excellent books available on intuition, exceptional dreams, dream incubation, and lucid dreaming. not mentioned here.

Benjamin, Sheila. *"Visitations from the World Beyond."* In **Lucid Dreaming**, edited by Teresa Martin, 126 – 135. Windyville, MO: SOM Publishing, 2008.

Barrett, Deirdre. **The Committee of Sleep**. New York: Crown Publishing Group, 2001.

Bulkeley, Kelly and Bulkley, Patricia. **Dreaming Beyond Death**. Boston: Beacon Press, 2005.

Bulkeley, Kelly. **Transforming Dreams: Learning Spiritual Lessons from the Dreams You Never Forget**. New York: John Wiley and Sons, 2000.

Burch, Wanda. **She Who Dreams: A Journey into Healing through Dreamwork**. Novato, CA: New World Library, 2003.

Campbell, Jean. **Group Dreaming: Dreams to the Tenth Power**. Norfolk, VA: Wordminder Press, 2006.

Clark, Laurel. **Dharma: Finding Your Soul's Purpose**. Windyville, MO: SOM Publishing, 2004.

Clark, Laurel. **Karmic Healing**. Windyville, MO: SOM Publishing, 2000.

Clark, Laurel. **Shaping Your Life**. e-book, Windyville, MO: SOM Publishing, 2000.

Clark, Laurel. *"Spiritual Dreaming."* In **Lucid Dreaming**, op. cit., 4 – 22.

Clark, Laurel. **The Law of Attraction and Other Secrets of Visualization**. Windyville, MO: SOM Publishing, 2007.

Condron, Barbara. **The Dreamer's Dictionary**. Windyville, MO: SOM Publishing, 1994.

Garfield, Patricia. **Creative Dreaming**. New York: Simon and
Schuster, 1974.

Krippner, Stanley. **Extraordinary Dreams and How to Work
with Them**. Albany, NY: SUNY Press, 2001.

Kubler-Ross, Elisabeth. **On Death and Dying**. New York, NY:
Macmillan, 1969

Meier, C.A. **Healing Dream and Ritual: Ancient Incubation
and Modern Psychotherapy**. Daimon Verlag, 1989.
(originally published in German, 1949, and translated
into English under the title **Ancient Incubation and Modern**
Psychotherapy, 1967.)

Moody, Raymond A., Jr. **Life After Life**. Covington, GA:
Mockingbird Press, 1975.

Moody, Raymond A., Jr. "*Spiritual Reunion*." Interview with
Laurel Clark in Thresholds Quarterly, Vol. 12, No. 4, 1994,
published by SOM Publishing, Windyville, MO.

Reed, Henry. "*Dream Incubation: A Reconstruction of a
Ritual in Contemporary Form*." Journal of Humanistic
Psychology, Vol. 16, No. 4 (Fall 1976): 53 – 69.

Rhine, J.B. **Extra-Sensory Perception**. Branden Books, 1983.
(originally published in 1934.)

Rothermel, Jerry L. **Mechanics of Dreams**. e-book, Windyville, MO:
SOM Publishing, 1989.

Waggoner, Robert. **Lucid Dreaming: Gateway to the Inner Self**.
Needham, MA: Moment Point Press, 2009.

Ward Hill Lamon, *Recollections of Abraham Lincoln*, 1847-1885
(as reported on dreamtree.com website).

Websites used for reference:

C. G. Jung Foundation website,
http://www.cgjungny.org/jlinks.html

DreamsCloud, http://www.dreamscloud.com

International Association for the Study of Dreams,
http://www.asdreams.org

"*Inventions that Came in Dreams,*" http://dreamtraining.
blogspot.com/2010/12/inventions-that-came-in-dreams-
largest.html

Notes from a Dreamer on Dreaming, http://www.bobbieann.net

Ryan Hurd's dream blog, http://www.dreamstudies.org

School of Metaphysics, http://www.som.org

School of Metaphysics online dream study program,
http://www.dreamschool.org

The Dream Tree, http://www.dreamtree.com

The Dream Tribe, http://www.thedreamtribe.com

Additional titles available from SOM Publishing

Dr. Laurel Clark
Dharma: Finding Your Soul's Purpose	$10.00
Karmic Healing	$15.00
The Law of Attraction	
and Other Secrets of Visualization	$13.00

Dr. Barbara O'Guinn Condron
DREAMTIME: *Parables of Universal Law*	
while Down Under	$13.00
Every Dream Is about the Dreamer	$13.00
First Opinion: *Wholistic Health Care*	
in the 21st Century	$15.00
How to Raise an Indigo Child	$14.00
Kundalini Rising: *Mastering Your*	
Creative Energies	$13.00
Master Living	$18.00
Peace Making: *9 Lessons for Changing Yourself,*	
Your Relationships, & the World	$12.00
Spiritual Renaissance: *Elevating Your*	
Consciousness for the Common Good	$15.00
The Dreamer's Dictionary	$15.00
The Work of the Soul	$13.00
Uncommon Knowledge: *Past Life &*	
Health Readings	$13.00
Wisdom of Solomon	$15.00

Dr. Christine Madar
The Moon's Effect on Dreams	$10.00

Dr. Daniel Condron

2012, 2013, & Beyond Time	$15.00
Dreams of the Soul: *The Yogi Sutras*	
of Pantanjali	$13.00
Permanent Healing	$13.00
Still Mind, Present Moment, Open Heart	$15.00
Superconscious Meditation	$13.00
The Emptiness Sutra	$10.00
The Purpose of Life	$15.00
The Secret Code of Revelation	$15.00
The Tao Te Ching Interpreted & Explained	$15.00
The Universal Language of Mind: *Book of Matthew*	
Interpreted	$13.00
Universal Healing Truths	$15.00
Understanding Your Dreams	$5.00

Dr. Teresa Martin

Lucid Dreaming	$12.00

To order write:
>School of Metaphysics World Headquarters
>163 Moon Valley Road
>Windyville, Missouri 65783 U.S.A.

Enclose a check or money order payable in U.S. funds to SOM with any order. Please include $7.00 for postage and handling of books, $15.00 for international orders.

A complete catalogue of all book titles, audio lectures, music CD's and videos is available upon request.

www.som.org
www.dreamschool.org

email: som@som.org

About the School of Metaphysics

We invite you to become a special part of our efforts to aid in enhancing and quickening the process of spiritual growth and mental evolution of the people of the world. The School of Metaphysics, a not-for-profit educational and service organization, has been in existence for three decades. During that time, we have taught tens of thousands directly through our course of study in applied metaphysics. We have elevated the awareness of millions through the many services we offer.

If you would like to pursue the study of mind and the transformation of Self to a higher level of being and consciousness, you are invited to write to us at the School of Metaphysics World Headquarters in Windyville, Missouri 65783.

The heart of the School of Metaphysics is a four-tiered course of study in understanding the mind in order to know the Self. Lessons introduce you to the Universal Laws and Truths which guide spiritual and physical evolution. Consciousness is explored and developed through mental and spiritual disciplines which enhance your physical life and enrich your soul progression. For every concept there is a means to employ it through developing your own potential. Level One includes concentration, visualization (focused imagery), meditation, and control of life force and creative energies, all foundations for exploring the multidimensional Self.

Study centers are located throughout the Midwestern United States. If there is not a center near you, you can receive the first series of lessons through correspondence with a teacher at our headquarters.

As experts in the Universal Language of Mind, we teach how to remember and understand the inner communication received through dreams. We are the sponsors of the National Dream Hotline®, an annual educational service offered the last weekend in April.

For those desiring spiritual renewal, Spiritual Focus weekends at our Moon Valley Ranch on the College of Metaphysics campus in Missouri offer calmness and clarity. Each weekend focuses on intuitive research done specifically for you in your presence.

More than a traditional class or seminar, these gatherings are experiences in multidimensional awareness of who you are, why you are here, where you came from, and where you are going.

The Universal Hour of Peace was initiated by the School of Metaphysics on October 24, 1995 in conjunction with the 50th anniversary of the United Nations. We believe that peace on earth is an idea whose time has come. To realize this dream, we invite you to join with others throughout the world by dedicating your thoughts and actions to peace for one hour beginning at 11:30 p.m. December 31st into the first day of January each year. Living peaceably begins by thinking peacefully. The hour is highlighted with recitation of the Universal Peace Covenant (see next page), a document written by over two dozen spiritual teachers. Each year, we encourage people around the world to read the Covenant as they welcome the new year. During this time, students and faculty at the College of Metaphysics hold a 24 hour peace vigil in the world's Peace Dome. For more information, visit www.peacedome.org .

There is the opportunity to aid in the growth and fulfillment of our work. Donations supporting the expansion of the School of Metaphysics' efforts are a valuable way for you to aid humanity. As a not-for-profit publishing house, SOM Publishing is dedicated to the continuing publication of research that promote peace, understanding and good will for all of Mankind. It is dependent upon the kindness and generosity of sponsors to do so. Authors donate their work and receive no royalties. We have many excellent manuscripts awaiting a benefactor.

One hundred percent of the donations made to the School of Metaphysics are used to expand our services. The world's first Peace Dome located on our college campus was funded entirely by individual contributions. Presently, donations are being received for the Octagon, an international center for multi-dimensional living. Donations to the School of Metaphysics are tax-exempt under 501(c)(3) of the Internal Revenue Code. We appreciate your generosity. With the help of people like you, our dream of a place where anyone desiring Self awareness can receive education in mastering the mind, consciousness, and the Self will become a reality.

236

The Universal Peace Covenant

Peace is the breath of our spirit.
It wells up from within the depths of our being to refresh, to heal, to inspire.

Peace is our birthright.
Its eternal presence exists within us as a memory of where we have come from and as a vision of where we yearn to go.

Our world is in the midst of change.
For millennia, we have contemplated, reasoned, and practiced the idea of peace. Yet the capacity to sustain peace eludes us. To transcend the limits of our own thinking we must acknowledge that peace is more than the cessation of conflict. For peace to move across the face of the earth we must realize, as the great philosophers and leaders before us, that all people desire peace. We hereby acknowledge this truth that is universal. Now humanity must desire those things that make for peace.

We affirm that peace is an idea whose time has come.
We call upon humanity to stand united, responding to the need for peace. We call upon each individual to create and foster a personal vision for peace. We call upon each family to generate and nurture peace within the home. We call upon each nation to encourage and support peace among its citizens. We call upon each leader, be they in the private home, house of worship or place of labor, to be a living example of peace for only in this way can we expect peace to move across the face of the earth.

World Peace begins within ourselves.
Arising from the spirit peace seeks expression through the mind, heart, and body of each individual. Government and laws cannot heal the heart. We must transcend whatever separates us. Through giving love and respect, dignity and comfort, we come to know peace. We learn to love our neighbors as we love ourselves bringing peace into the world. We hereby commit ourselves to this noble endeavor.

Peace is first a state of mind. *Peace affords the greatest opportunity for growth and learning which leads to personal happiness. Self-direction promotes inner peace and therefore leads to outer peace. We vow to heal ourselves through forgiveness, gratitude, and prayer. We commit to causing each and every day to be a fulfillment of our potential, both human and divine.*

Peace is active, the motion of silence, of faith, of accord, of service. *It is not made in documents but in the minds and hearts of men and women. Peace is built through communication. The open exchange of ideas is necessary for discovery, for well-being, for growth, for progress whether within one person or among many. We vow to speak with sagacity, listen with equanimity, both free of prejudice, thus we will come to know that peace is liberty in tranquility.*

Peace is achieved by those who fulfill their part of a greater plan. *Peace and security are attained by those societies where the individuals work closely to serve the common good of the whole. Peaceful coexistence between nations is the reflection of man's inner tranquility magnified. Enlightened service to our fellowman brings peace to the one serving, and to the one receiving. We vow to live in peace by embracing truths that apply to us all.*

Living peaceably begins by thinking peacefully.
We stand on the threshold of peace-filled understanding. We come together, all of humanity, young and old of all cultures from all nations. We vow to stand together as citizens of the Earth, knowing that every question has an answer, every issue a resolution. As we stand, united in common purpose, we hereby commit ourselves in thought and action so we might know the power of peace in our lifetimes.

Peace be with us all ways.

May Peace Prevail On Earth.

created by teachers in the School of Metaphysics 1996-1997